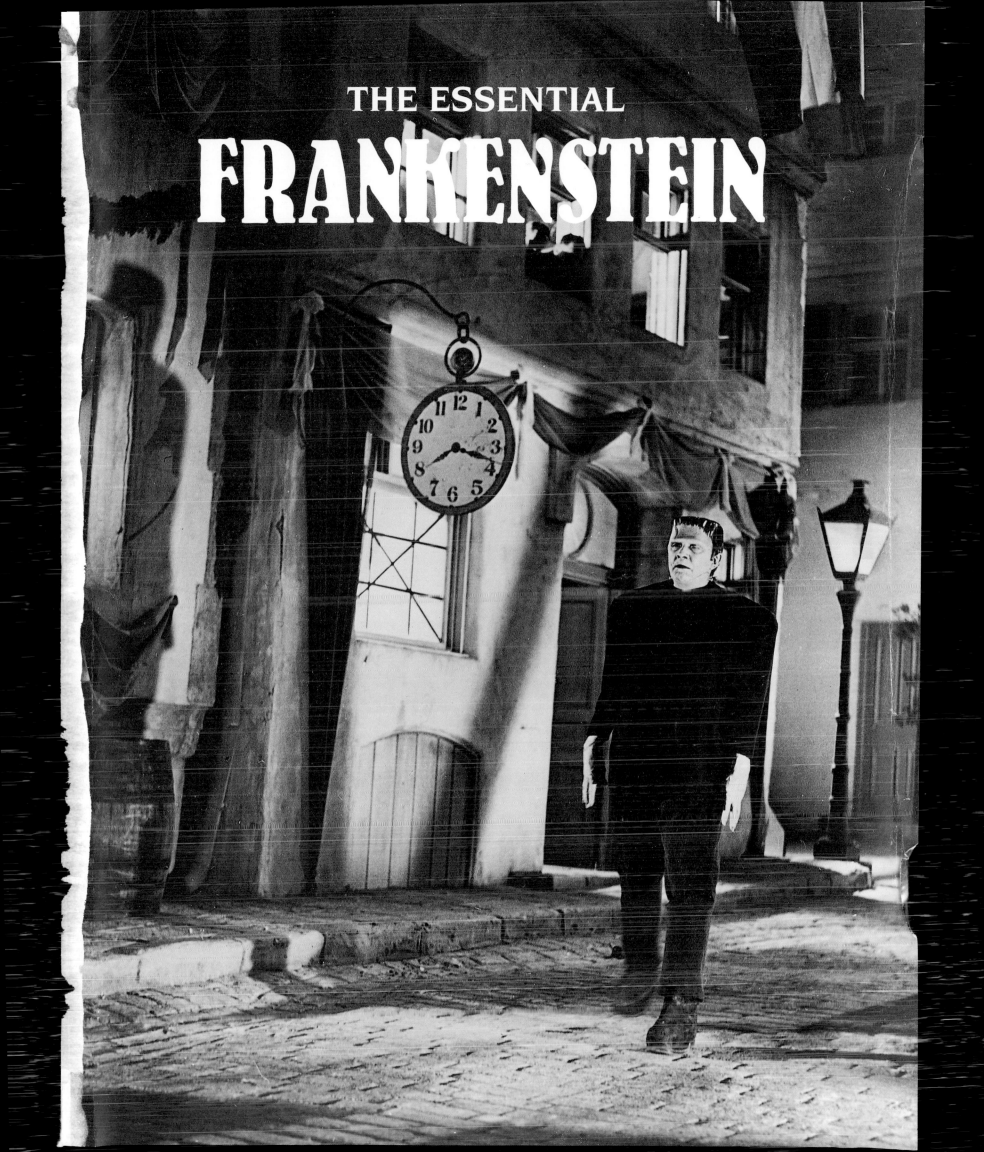

THE ESSENTIAL
FRANKENSTEIN

THE ESSENTIAL
FRANKENSTEIN

by Robert Jameson

Crescent Books
New York

This 1992 edition published by Crescent Books, distributed by Outlet Book Company, Inc., a Random House Company, 40 Engelhard Avenue Avenel, New Jersey 07001

Produced by Brompton Books Corporation 15 Sherwood Place, Greenwich, CT 06830

ISBN 0-517-06974-1

8 7 6 5 4 3 2 1

Printed and bound in Hong Kong

Page 1: *Glenn Strange stalks the streets in* Frankenstein Meets the Wolf Man (1943).

Page 2-3: *Peter Cushing confronts his creation in Hammer's* The Evil of Frankenstein (1964).

Right: *Frankenstein's son (Basil Rathbone) reanimates his father's monster in* Son of Frankenstein (1939).

Contents

The Spark of Life

How 'a young girl came to think of and to dilate

upon so very hideous an idea.'

MARY SHELLEY, PREFACE TO *Frankenstein*

Every tribe on earth has a creation story. The Jews and the Christians have the story as told in the book of Genesis; the Aborigines tell of 'The Dreaming'; while the early Egyptians were convinced that mankind was formed from the tears of the Sun God, Ra.

These tales have something in common – they are all extremely ancient. It seems that wherever in the world they wandered, humans asked each other one question before all others: how did we come to exist?

The answers to this question that satisfied people most deeply were composed long before writing was invented. The epic creation stories have thus come down to us complete, and yet mysterious, transmitted across the ages by dance, poetry, painting and song, so that we can never know quite how they began, or who was responsible for their sublime imagination.

Except in one instance. For what is *Frankenstein* if it is not simply the newest creation story? The creation story of a scientific, rather than religious, world. Its story – of how one individual usurps the role of God by creating another being, and how that being, cut off from divine or human friendship, is corrupted by its terrible loneliness – seems to touch some profound chord in the modern psyche. This is surely proven by *Frankenstein*'s ubiquitous appeal. The myth has infiltrated every conceivable medium, from novel, play, and poem, to film, video and rock song.

Yet there is one essential difference between our modern creation myth and its ancient predecessors. For the ancient stories were designed to satisfy curiosity and to bestow upon the listener a sense of belonging and wonder. Whereas *Frankenstein* is a tale of darkness, intended to sow the seeds of

Left: *Mary Shelley, painted by Richard Rothwell c. 1840, over 20 years after her initial success with Frankenstein.*

Above: *Percy Bysshe Shelley, the radical poet, whose relationship with Mary Godwin was legalized only a few months before the publication of his wife's novel.*

nature, and after Fanny's father deserted her she jumped off London's Putney Bridge – only to be fished out of the river by some rather suprised Thames boatmen. Like Godwin, she professed to despise marriage as 'legalized prostitution,' and both the lovers had some explaining to do to their radical friends when they decided to get married after Mary became pregnant in 1797.

Mary Shelley was never to know her extraordinary mother. Mary Wollstonecraft died of an infection contracted as a direct result of giving birth to her daughter. (Indeed, some academics have argued that Mary Shelley's fascination with the creation of a parentless monster may have been a result of her latent guilt about her mother's death.) Although as a child Mary adored her father, the busy and rather distant William Godwin was well aware of his shortcomings as a parent. In 1801 he remarried, providing Mary and Fanny with a stepmother, Mrs Clairemont, and an extended family in the form of his new wife's two children, Charles and Jane (later known as Claire). Despite the enlarged household, Mary felt an intense loneliness as a child. This craving for companionship was later to entirely dominate the character of her most famous creation – Frankenstein's monster. But in Mary it formed the vulnerable part of a personality that her father described as 'singularly bold, somewhat imperious . . . and in perseverance almost invincible.'

Mary intensely disliked her stepmother, and she spent much of the period between 1812 and 1814 staying with family friends in Scotland. It was on her return to London after this sojourn that she came to know a young poet and admirer of

doubt and to fill the listener's mind with . . . *horror*.

The story of the creation of the novel *Frankenstein* is almost as fascinating and bizarre a saga as that of the creation of the monster itself. It is a tale that involves two of the greatest poets in the English language, Percy Shelley and Lord Byron, and a host of other strange and tragic characters. But most of all, of course, it is the story of the early years of Mary Shelley, author of *Frankenstein*, who between the age of 16 and 25 lived what she herself called 'an incarnate Romance.'

Mary seems to have been destined for an extraordinary life from the moment of her conception. Her parents were both famous intellectuals, admired by free thinkers such as William Wordsworth and Samuel Taylor Coleridge, but despised by much of London Society as immoral atheists.

Mary's father was the radical philosopher William Godwin, who was revered by contemporaries as one of the finest minds of the age. In works such as *Political Justice*, published in 1793, he railed against the restraints placed on individuals by marriage, by government, and by religious taboos. Godwin's rationalist philosophy greatly influenced his daughter, and his firm belief that girls ought to be educated as thoroughly as boys meant that from an early age Mary was encouraged to read ambitiously.

If anything, London found Mary Shelley's mother even more startling than her father. Mary Wollstonecraft was a notable early feminist who became somewhat notorious after the publication of her *Vindication of the Rights of Women* in 1792. Before she met Godwin she had already had a child, Fanny, by a previous lover. Mary Wollstonecraft had a passionate

her father, Percy Bysshe Shelley.

By this point in his life Shelley, aged 22 and heir to a baronetcy and a large fortune, had begun to prove his literary genius with poems such as *Queen Mab* (1813). He had also determined upon a life as a free spirit, and his passionate and romantic nature had already led him into a series of difficulties. Expelled from Oxford in 1811 after publishing *The Necessity For Atheism*, he soon after eloped with a 16-year-old beauty, Harriet Westbrook.

In the following years Harriet was dragged through a series of madcap adventures, including ineffectual attempts to help emancipate Ireland and to set up a commune in Wales. As a known radical Shelley was sometimes spied upon by government agents, and he claimed to have been the near-victim of an assasination attempt. In many respects Shelley, with his wild enthusiasms and visionary ideals, formed the prototype for Victor Frankenstein, creator of the monster.

Shelley quickly grew bored of Harriet, and by the summer of 1814 he felt no compunction at falling in love with the 16 year old Mary Godwin. Mary returned Shelley's advances with enthusiasm, taking him on long melancholy walks to the graveyard at St Pancras where her adored mother was buried. One sunny day in June, standing beside her mother's grave, Mary declared her absolute love for Shelley and offered herself to him unconditionally.

Unfortunately it transpired that while Godwin advocated a radical lifestyle in principle, he wanted to postpone such experiences for his teenage daughter. The next few weeks at the Godwin home were fraught, to say the least, with Shelley at one point forcing himself into the house to offer Mary a bottle of laudanum while shouting, 'They wish to separate us, my love; but Death shall unite us.'

Shelley, of course, had already discovered the answer to difficult parents. In July 1814 the lovers eloped to the Continent, with Mrs Godwin in frantic but useless pursuit. During this elopement the couple (who were accompanied, in a fit of conspiratorial excitement, by Mary's step-sister Claire) enjoyed a voyage down the picturesque Rhine valley, passing within a few miles of the castle once owned by the medieval family of Frankenstein; it seems probable that this was when Mary took note of the name.

Returning to England after two months abroad, the elopers found that the anger of their respective families had hardly abated. Furthermore, Shelley was pursued by creditors, and Mary discovered that she was pregnant with her first child. Mary's child was born premature in early 1815 and died after only ten days; she wrote in her journal how she had dreamed that the baby had not quite died, and that she had been able to warm it to life beside the fire.

Meanwhile Claire hatched a scheme that was to lead to the creation of *Frankenstein*. There is no doubt that Claire was frantically jealous of Mary's relationship with Shelley, whose literary star was burning ever brighter. So, with a shamelessness that has to be admired, she set about finding herself an even more eminent lover.

At the time there was no more notorious a character in London society than the poet Lord Byron. Claire began shadowing Byron to his favorite theaters, and one night sent a

provocative note to his box, entreating him to meet her. After a short period of wooing – on Claire's part, not Byron's – Byron took her to his bed. He never pretended to love her, however, and was later to defend his actions by saying that it was not reasonable to expect a man to resist a pretty young girl who made all the advances herself and at the same time gave assurances that she knew everything there was to know about birth control. Of course, within a few months Claire was pregnant. Byron meanwhile, hounded by creditors and by shocking rumors about his bisexuality and his dubious relationship with his sister, was forced to make a wild flight across Europe, whipping his coach-horses through the muddy lanes of France. He was never to return to England.

Most young women of the period would have gone into a decline at this point, but Claire was made of sterner stuff. She immediately persuaded the Shelleys that they should all spend the summer in Geneva, which she knew would bring her into conjunction with Byron's continental orbitings.

Thus it was that the Shelley entourage, with the addition of baby William, who had been born to Mary early in 1816, set off for the Alps – the future homeland of Frankenstein and his monstrous creation.

We know from Mary's journals that she found her Alpine summer of 1816 both happy and exciting. She adored her new

Left, right and below right: *The story of how Mary Shelley dreamed up the idea of Frankenstein is as famous as the tale itself. The gathering of characters as exotic as Byron, his doctor Polidori, and Percy and Mary Shelley has been the subject of several films: Haunted Summer (left), Gothic (right) and Frankenstein: The True Story (below right).*

son, she was away from her unforgiving father, and Shelley's money problems had been solved by the gleefully welcomed news of his grandfather's death. Furthermore, when Shelley first met Byron in Geneva the two men formed an immediate and enduring friendship (the only point of contention being Claire, whom Byron continued to treat with contempt until bedtime).

It was soon agreed that Byron would rent the opulent Villa Diodati in Geneva, overlooking the lake, while Shelley would take the humbler Maison Chapuis nearby. All through the summer there was a constant toing and froing between the two houses. Byron and Shelley sailed boats on the lake, and Mary joined them in expeditions to sights such as the glacier at Chamonix, which was to provide such a dramatic setting for Frankenstein's first conversation with his Monster.

On one overcast and stormy evening both households congregated in the Villa Diodati to read a volume of German ghost stories. Gathered around a great log fire in the main living room were Mary, Shelley, Byron, Claire and a certain Dr Polidori. (Polidori, whom Byron had brought with him to tend to his piles and various sexual diseases, tragically committed suicide a few years later by swallowing a vast quantity of Prussic acid [hydrogen cyanide] in a fit of gloom.) When they had exhausted the chilling tales, silence descended on the company, until Byron exclaimed, 'We will each write a ghost story!'

So, over the next few days, each participant tried to conjure up something suitably petrifying. Shelley's attempt was a soon-forgotten tale based on his childhood; Byron's was more notable, being a story about a vampire, which was later completed and published by Polidori; while Polidori's was a rather ridiculous offering about a skull-headed woman who peeped through keyholes. Mary meanwhile busied herself to think of a story 'to make the reader dread to look around, to curdle the blood.'

For many days her powers of invention deserted her, but

Left: *Geneva as Mary Shelley would have known it. The romantic landscape around the town, with its lakes, forests, mountains, and glaciers provided the dramatic setting for Mary's tale of horror and tragedy.*

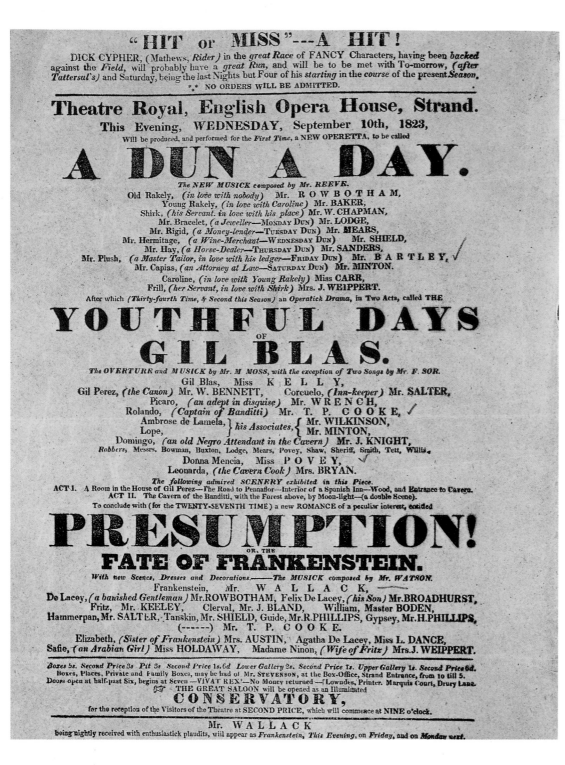

Left: *The novel Frankenstein was an immediate success. Within five years of publication, Frankenstein was adapted for the stage and played to London audiences lured by the thrill of gothic horror.*

then one evening she sat listening to a conversation between Byron and Shelley concerning the 'nature of the principle of life.' The two poets even wondered whether one day 'a corpse would be reanimated.'

Shelley had always been fascinated by science: his student rooms at Oxford had been littered with experimental equipment. We know from Mary Shelley's introduction to the 1831 edition of her novel that she listened intently while the poet discussed the findings of Luigi Galvani, the great Italian physiologist. Galvani had discovered in 1791 that a dead frog's leg would twitch when touched by two different types of metal, though he did not understand the nature of the electrical current that gave this effect.

It seems likely that at this point Polidori, who had recently graduated from the famous medical school at Edinburgh,

interjected what he knew about the work of Giovanni Aldini, nephew of Galvani. Aldini, not content with dead frogs, had 'galvanized' the heads of decapitated oxen, and had succeeded in making their ears shake, tongues loll and eyes roll. In 1803 Aldini graduated to humans, when he was permitted to electrify the corpse of a hanged murderer at Newgate Prison in London. The next year he repeated the grisly experiment using a more powerful charge, and a witness reported that the cadaver even seemed to lift itself and clench its fists.

In fact, electrifying corpses was a surprisingly common pastime. The anatomist Xavier Bichat was lucky enough to be living in Revolutionary Paris during 'The Terror,' and was thus able to pluck hundreds of freshly severed aristocratic heads from the baskets of Madame Guillotine. He subjected these noble heads to various indignities, including electrification

to see if their ears would waggle.

That night, after hearing Byron and Shelley enthusiastically discussing all this, Mary found it difficult to sleep. Her imagination ran riot, and she fell into what she later described as a 'waking dream' about a ghastly experiment:

> I saw the pale student of the unhallowed arts kneeling beside the thing he had put together. I saw the hideous phantasm of a man stretched out, and then, on the working of some powerful engine, show signs of life, and stir with an uneasy, half-vital motion.

Mary also imagined the horror of the creator of the monster on realizing his fatal success. She dreamed of the scientist falling into an exhausted slumber, only to be awakened by the horrid thing standing by his bedside, 'opening his curtains and looking on him with yellow, watery, but speculative eyes.'

At this point Mary frightened herself so much that she woke up with a start. But her fear turned to elation as she realized that she had invented her ghost story, and she whispered exultantly to herself in the dark, 'What terrified me will terrify others!'

Mary conceived the main themes of *Frankenstein* during her Alpine holiday, but she actually wrote most of the book in the gentler surroundings of Bath, in England. When the Geneva house parties broke up Byron departed for Italy, while Mary escorted Claire back to the spa town so that she could give birth to Byron's illegitimate child in decent obscurity.

Mary's stay in Bath was relatively peaceful, and allowed her to do some background reading in the form of Sir Humphry Davy's standard textbook on chemistry. (Davy, incidentally, was the tutor of the greatest early experimenter with electricity, Michael Faraday.)

While Mary and Shelley were in Bath a double tragedy overtook them. Mary's half-sister, Fanny, who had always been prone to melancholy and had been rather abused as the go-between in the continuing battle between Mary and her father, committed suicide. Soon afterwards Shelley received the news that his first wife, the tragic Harriet Westbrook, had drowned herself in the Serpentine. Mary found these deaths deeply disturbing, and at certain points in her novel the neurotic scientist Frankenstein seems to express her feelings of guilt and emotional confusion.

In an unsuccessful attempt to gain custody of Harriet's children, Mary and Shelley married in late 1817 – and thus the author of Frankenstein is recorded as Mary Shelley rather than Mary Godwin. The novel was completed in the quiet town of Marlow in May, and published on 11 March 1818. At the age of 20, Mary had written what was to become the most famous horror story of all time.

Mary Shelley begins her story in the form of letters written by a mysterious explorer, Robert Walton, to his sister just as he embarks on a dangerous voyage to the Arctic. Early in the voyage Walton spies a gigantic creature speeding along an iceflow on a sledge. Soon after, his ship rescues a terribly exhausted man from a drifting iceberg. The stranger, who is of course the scientist Frankenstein, recognizes Walton as a kindred spirit and relates to him his tragic personal history.

It transpires that Frankenstein led a relatively happy childhood, in a country house his prosperous parents owned outside Geneva, on the shore of the lake. Frankenstein's mother died when he was young, but he was consoled by the companionship of his adopted sister, Elizabeth, and was able to pursue an early passion for alchemy.

The story describes Frankenstein's childhood wish to 'learn the hidden laws of nature,' and tells of how eventually the young Frankenstein enrolls at the University of Ingolstadt as a student of Natural Science. There he astonishes his professors by his dedication and becomes devoted to discovering the 'principle of life.' To this end he happily spends 'days and nights in vaults and charnel houses.'

The young Frankenstein becomes obsessed with the idea of creating a human being, and decides to make this being eight feet tall in order to overcome the problem of fashioning the minutest parts. After spending months closeted in his attic study, shunning his fellow students as if he had been 'guilty of a crime,' and collecting raw materials from 'the dissecting room and the slaughter house,' all that remains for him to do is to 'infuse a spark of being into the lifeless thing.' However, after he sees 'the dull yellow eye of the creature open,' Frankenstein is seized by horror and disgust. He paces his rooms, uncertain of what to do, until he falls into a fitful sleep. When he awakes, the creature is gone.

For months Frankenstein succumbs to a nervous illness. When he recovers it is only to find that the creature has begun to wreak vengeance on its creator. Back at the family home, Frankenstein's young brother William is murdered, and worse, a trusted maid, Justine, is accused of the killing. After seeing the monster on the shores of the lake while journeying home, Frankenstein realizes that his creation committed the crime. But he is at first unwilling, and then unable, to convince anyone.

Following Justine's execution, Frankenstein is overwhelmed by guilt, and bears 'a hell within . . . that nothing can extinguish.' He finds peace only in the wilds of Nature, but on a trip across the glacier at Chamonix the monster approaches him and forces Frankenstein to listen to a description of how he has spent his first year.

The creature describes his sensations upon waking: how he spent his first few days in a forest, surviving on nuts and berries and gradually coming to understand the natural world around him. The first man he encountered, however, ran shrieking from him in horror, and when he stumbled into a village he was chased away like a wild beast. Taking refuge in a

Above left: One of the earliest illustrations of Frankenstein.

Above: The Hammer film studios produced one of the most effective laboratory sets for The Evil of Frankenstein. Here Peter Cushing as Frankenstein, toils over his masterpiece 'to infuse a spark of being into the lifeless thing.'

Right, top and above: The monster first met his creator on the Chamonix Glacier, a setting obviously inspired by Shelley's sojourn in Switzerland during the summer of 1816. Frankenstein and his creation journeyed to the Orkney Islands to build the monster a companion.

hovel, he was able secretly to watch the lives of the poverty stricken family living in the adjacent cottage. From listening to them, the creature learned to speak, and began to understand the ways of mankind. He also came to understand how ugly he was, and though this filled him with the 'bitterest sensations' it did not at first corrupt him. He continued to do good deeds for his unwitting benefactors, such as stealthily cutting wood for them. The creature even discovered some books and taught himself to read. (Horror film fans may be surprised to learn that in the first few months of his existence their 'monster' could be accurately described as a French-speaking vegetarian with a passion for Milton.) This strange idyll ended when the monster introduced himself to one of the cottagers – a blind old man. Unfortunately the old man's family returned unexpectedly and attacked the creature. His only hope of friendship lost forever, the monster vowed 'an everlasting war against the human species,' and especially against his creator.

As he made his way back to the environs of the Frankenstein home, the monster saved a drowning girl, but was attacked by hunters. Filled with new anger, he happened on Frankenstein's little brother William, and committed his first murder. His heart 'swelled with exaltation and hellish

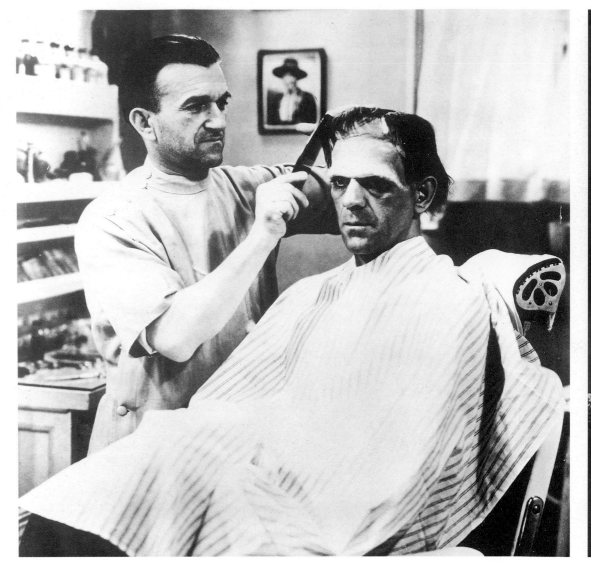

triumph.' Chancing upon Justine sleeping in a barn, the creature demonstrated his cunning by 'planting' a piece of the
child's jewelry upon her: an act of malignity inspired by his
bitterness that a girl as lovely as she would never look upon
him with anything but horror.

The monster ends his monologue by claiming that it is his
terrible solitude that has turned him to evil, and demanding
that Frankenstein should create a second monster as
'deformed and horrible as himself.' The scientist at first re-
coils in horror at the suggestion, but by using a mixture of
threats to Frankenstein's family, and promises to live with his
mate in some foreign wilderness, the creature gains his
creator's acquiescence.

Frankenstein departs for Britain with an old friend, Henry
Clerval, in order to do some necessary research. The scientist
eventually journeys up to the Orkney Islands off the north
Scottish coast – a suitably dreary wasteland in which to resume his diabolical work. However, when the 'mate' is still
only half-built he begins to regret the promise he has made,
and fears that the two monsters will breed a race of horrors
that will plague mankind. When the monster appears at his
cottage window, Frankenstein destroys its ghastly bride
before its eyes.

While he is dumping the half-finished female monster at
sea, Frankenstein's sailing boat is blown by a gale to Ireland.

There he discovers that the monster's dreadful revenge has been to strangle Henry Clerval. Frankenstein is accused of Clerval's murder, but eventually proves his innocence.

Racked by a now intolerable guilt, Frankenstein travels back to Geneva to fulfill his old promise to marry Elizabeth. On their wedding night, however, he leaves Elizabeth alone for a moment, only to return to see the creature jeering at him through the window of the bridal suite, 'as with his fiendish finger he pointed towards the corpse of my wife.'

When Frankenstein returns to the family home with the news, his father promptly dies of grief. The tormented scientist then vows on the family tomb to track and destroy his creation, a vow that eventually brings him to the far North and to his meeting with Walton.

Having told his story, the dying Frankenstein at first begs Walton to learn from it, and to 'seek happiness in tranquility and avoid ambition.' But as he expires he exclaims 'Yet why do I say this . . . another may succeed!'

The novel ends with Walton discovering the monster paying his last respects to the corpse of his creator. The monster seems to regret the pain he has caused, and in a sad little epitaph he explains to the explorer that he is about to travel to the North Pole, where he will collect his own funeral pyre. His final act of violence will be to burn his own body so that no-one can ever make another like him.

Above: *The monster makes off with Frankenstein's lovely young bride.*

Frankenstein goes to Hollywood

'His face fascinated me. I made drawings of his head,

adding sharp bony ridges where I imagined

the skull might have joined.'

JAMES WHALE ON BORIS KARLOFF

The phenomenal success of the novel *Frankenstein* when it was first published prompted a flood of adaptations for the theater. The first, entitled *Presumption; or, The Fate of Frankenstein*, opened at the English Opera House in London in 1823. The play, which was a great success, was seen by Mary Shelley herself, who describes in her correspondence the 'breathless eagerness of the audience'.

The plot had to be severely compressed, and the dénouement consisted of the burial of Frankenstein and his creation under an avalanche. The play was revived in 1826, when the monster was killed off in a shipwreck instead. It seems that even this early, visualizers of the story were being tempted to add a little physical drama to the tragic intensity of the novel's climax.

The first foreign production of *Frankenstein* was staged in Paris in 1826. Entitled '*Le monstre et le magicien*,' this was a distinctly perverse version of the story, with the monster created by black magic, but destroyed by a lightning bolt. Indeed, 1826 was a vintage year for *Frankenstein* productions, with multiple stagings in London and other major towns. 'Frankomania' was born.

Left: *Frankenstein's monster in classic form. Boris Karloff in the 1931 movie.*

Right: *The first foreign theater production was* Le monstre et le magicien, *staged in Paris in 1825, with Thomas Cooke as the monster.*

The EDISON KINETOGRAM

VOL. 1   LONDON, APRIL 15, 1910   No. 1

SCENE FROM

FRANKENSTEIN

FILM No. 6604

EDISON FILMS TO BE RELEASED FROM MAY 11 TO 18 INCLUSIVE

writer decided to use that old horror cliche 'it had all been a dream' rather than provide a suitably tragic climax.

Although America can claim to have produced the first two *Frankenstein* films, the real inspiration for Universal's later, classic, *Frankenstein* lies with the early horror movies of Germany. The artistic and commercial success of early German films such as the *Student of Prague* (1913), in which a man sold his doppelgänger or double to the Devil, led to a silent horror genre that thrived until the coming of Fascism in the 1930s.

The earliest German film that directly influenced Frankenstein films is *The Cabinet of Dr Caligari*, made in 1919. The film is about an evil hypnotist working in a fair, who sends one of the fair's exhibits, a 'sleeping man,' off on murderous errands. In the most famous scene the somnambulist, chased by angry townsfolk, carries a swooning heroine across the countryside. The film was extremely influential in its use of Expressionist-style film sets, which provide striking nightmarish backdrops to the action. A similar mix of dramatic shadow, angular lines and distorted shapes was used to great effect in the Universal *Frankenstein* series – most notably in *Son of Frankenstein*.

Another German movie that impressed later film-makers was the 1920 version of *Der Golem*. Made by Paul Wegener, this film was inspired by the old Jewish legend that related how a huge clay statue was brought to life in sixteenth-century Prague by a rabbi to protect his community from a pogrom. The statue, or golem, eventually runs out of control and has to be rendered harmless by a little girl, who succeeds in removing the life-giving Star of David from its breast. Apart from the obvious monster-runs-amok parallels, Boris Karloff, the most famous Universal monster of all, once remarked that he had copied his monster's walk from the stiff-backed gait of the clay golem.

It is interesting that many of the plot twists and distortions beloved of Hollywood were actually invented in these early stage adaptations. For example, the 1826 Royal Coburg Theatre production introduced the idea of vigilante peasants chasing the monster across the countryside. 'Funny Frankensteins' were also produced remarkably early, and show the same play on names that characterize later film comedies. *Frank-in-Steam*, put on in London in 1823, was a typical burlesque version of the saga in that its plot revolved around the idea of someone mistakenly thinking that they had revived a corpse.

Frankenstein has the honor of being the subject of the first horror movie ever made. Admittedly this first version, made by Edison Studios in 1910, was silent and ran for only ten minutes. The actor who played the monster, Charles Ogle, created his own make-up – though this was more extraordinary than terrifying in its effect. It could be argued that Ogle's is not only the earliest but also the silliest monster ever created. However, in many ways, with its staring eyes and ragged appearance, this monster is closer to Mary Shelley's conception than the more finished creations of the later films.

In 1915 the Ocean Film Corporation also made a silent version of the *Frankenstein* legend, eschewing the obvious title in favor of the rather pedantic *Life Without Soul*. The title is not the worst thing about this movie, for in the last reel the script

Left: *The first horror film ever made was* Frankenstein, *produced in 1910 by the Edison Studios.*

Below: *The malign influence of a scientist over his creature was a popular theme.* The Cabinet of Dr Caligari, *released in 1919, used striking Expressionist sets to create an unsettling atmosphere. The film greatly influenced horror film directors of the 1930s.*

Right: Der Golem *recounted an ancient Jewish legend about a statue animated by a rabbi to protect his town from a pogrom. The 1931* Frankenstein *uses several of the themes from this film, but more importantly, Boris Karloff said he copied the Golem's stiff-backed walk.*

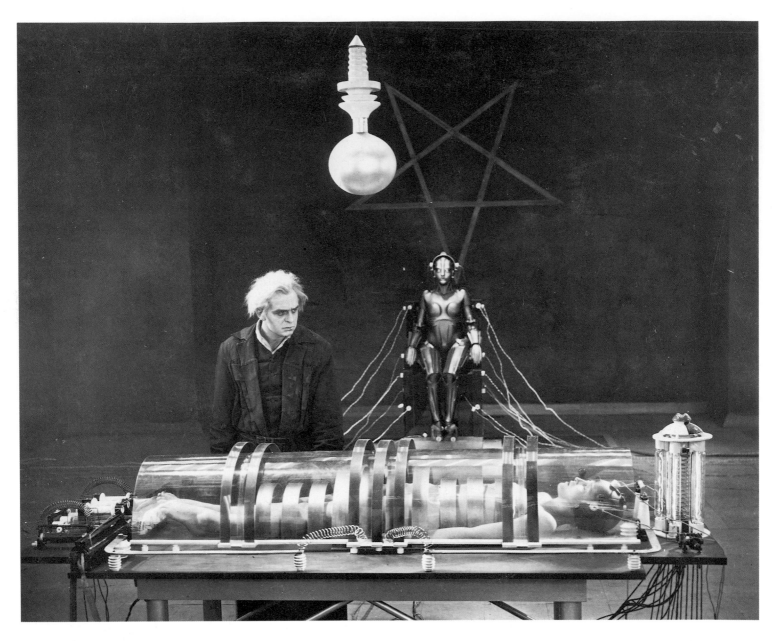

It is known that James Whale, director of the first two Universal *Frankensteins*, deliberately viewed a number of German horror films to gain inspiration. These included *The Cabinet of Dr Caligari* and Fritz Lang's classic *Metropolis* (1926). Although the marvelous electrical laboratory featured in *Metropolis* surely made an impression on Whale, another film entitled *The Magician*, directed by Rex Ingram in 1926, seems to have had a more direct impact. *The Magician* was a stylish movie that contained sequences shot in a striking tower laboratory; it also featured a memorable dwarf assistant.

The story of the making of the classic *Frankenstein* series cannot be separated from the story of the studio that created it, and which the series, in turn, repeatedly saved from bankruptcy. Universal Studios was founded in 1914 by Carl Laemmle, a German by birth who was well aware of the German horror tradition. Laemmle had owned an earlier film company, the Chicago-based Independent Motion Pictures, which had made a version of *Dr Jekyll and Mr Hyde*.

Laemmle was a hard-nosed studio mogul, and to begin with Universal made its money churning out unadventurous but reasonably profitable comedies and dramas. In 1923 the actor Lon Chaney helped to establish the studio as a horror-producer with his famous version of *The Hunchback of Notre Dame*. Chaney was known as a master of bizarre make-up, and in 1925 Laemmle decided to cash in on the success of *Hunchback* with a version of *The Phantom of the Opera*. This rather patchy movie is remembered as a classic largely because of Chaney's deliciously cadaverous performance, which was so successful that the actor was tempted away by MGM in the year it was released.

By now Laemmle had begun to scent the profits to be made out of horror. He imported the German director, Paul Leni, who had made a reputation for himself with macabre films such as *Waxworks* (1924). It was Leni who fully established the horror genre at Universal, but most importantly, it was his influence that ensured that horror directors at Universal would be allowed to be stylistically innovative in their cinematography and set design.

On 28 April 1929, Laemmle presented his son, Carl Laemmle Jr., with an extraordinary 21st birthday present. Carl Jr. was to be Universal Studio's Vice President in Charge of Production. This cavalier decision by Laemmle was to bring the studio close to ruin, yet during Carl Jr.'s short reign (he never produced another picture after the age of 28) Universal released a matchless string of Hollywood classics, including the greatest anti-war film of all, *All Quiet on the Western Front*.

The first major horror film Universal made under Carl Jr.'s stewardship was the classic *Dracula* (1931). Originally this was to have been a vehicle for Lon Chaney, but Chaney's death from throat cancer left the star role open for Bela Lugosi, who was later to be Boris Karloff's chief rival as the star of Hollywood horror.

Dracula was a great commercial success, and Carl Jr. immediately began to cast around for a horror sequel. He hired a talented young director, Robert Florey, to find a suitable screenplay. Florey considered various classic stories, including *Murders on the Rue Morgue* and *The Invisible Man*, before settling on Mary Shelley's *Frankenstein*.

Florey himself wrote a screenplay for the film, but the studio also bought the rights to a contemporary *Frankenstein* stage play written by Peggy Webling, and paid another writer, John Balderston, to adapt the play for the screen. The final screenplay is thus a collage of ideas brought together from all these various sources by the eventual director of the film, James Whale.

The story of how Whale, rather than Florey, came to direct *Frankenstein* is characteristic of the studio intrigues and general double-dealing that surrounded the making of the *Frankenstein* series. Carl Jr. had originally promised Florey that he would both write and direct. When the studio began to use other screenwriters on the script, Florey grew suspicious

Left: *Fritz Lang's futuristic masterpiece* Metropolis (1926) *shared a number of themes with the* Frankenstein *story and inspired Universal's producers when they worked on the 1931* Frankenstein.

Above right: *Carl Laemmle Sr. with his son Carl Jr. At the age of 21 Carl Jr. was put in charge of Universal, the studio founded by his father, and was responsible for a number of Hollywood classics, among them* Frankenstein.

Right: *A still from Rex Ingram's* The Magician (1926). *With a stunning laboratory in a tower, and a sinister hunchbacked assistant, it undoubtedly influenced the directors of Universal's* Frankenstein *movies.*

Left: *The British director of the first two Universal Frankensteins, James Whale. He was an extremely talented director, whose attention to detail turned* Frankenstein *into a classic.*

and demanded a written contract stipulating that he would have full control. The studio provided him with this, but they cunningly left out of the contract the name of the film he was to have control over. Thus, when Florey ran into early production problems, the studio simply passed the whole project over to another director, James Whale – who, in a fit of pique, refused even to give Florey a screenwriter's credit.

The main difficulty Florey had to contend with can be summed up in two words – Bela Lugosi. Universal had decided to capitalize on the success of *Dracula* by giving

Lugosi the monster role in their next horror epic. Lugosi, however, who had been enjoying a stream of passionate fan mail after his sexy and distinguished role as Count Dracula, immediately took against a part that meant disfiguring his patrician features with make-up and speaking in no more than a grunt. He was unhelpful to Universal's chief make-up man, Jack Pierce, who eventually based his creation on the monster in *Der Golem*. Unfortunately when Carl Jr. saw the first tests he simply laughed. Fortunately, Lugosi rejected the part, and Carl Jr., worried about the amount of time that was

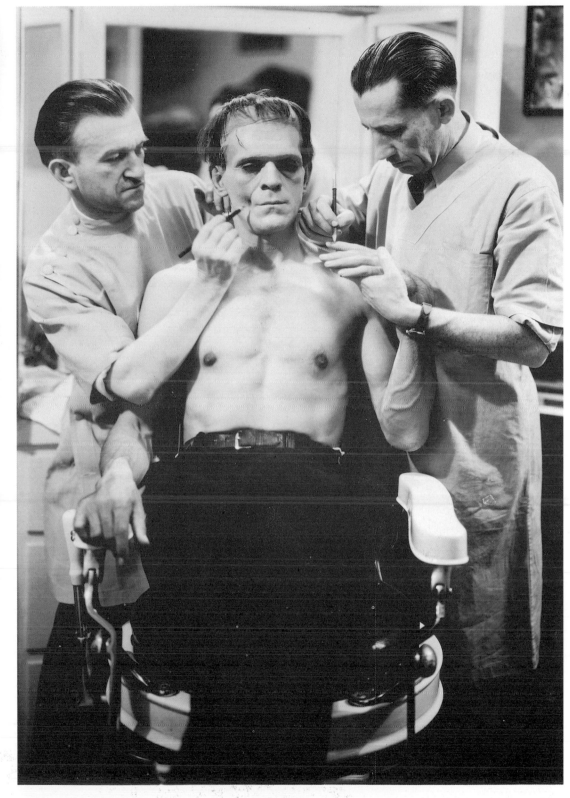

Above and right: *How to produce a monstrously successful movie. Laboring under heavy make-up and a weighty costume, Karloff was not comfortable during filming, which took place at the height of the Californian summer.*

being wasted, hired James Whale as director.

Few critics doubt that it was the brilliant, if egomaniacal, talent of James Whale that turned *Frankenstein* into a true classic. Whale immediately began deep discussions with Jack Pierce on the concept that should lie behind the make-up. They agreed that the monster needed a 'pathetic' side to his character, though the studio would have been happier with a simple rampaging monster.

Pierce researched his design for weeks, eventually deciding on the crucial shape of the monster's head after realizing that as Victor Frankenstein in the original novel was a scientist,

not a trained surgeon, he would have selected a large cranium and simply sawn it in half to give a lid-effect before popping the brain in. Incidentally, Pierce maintained that what most of the cinema audience interpreted as bolts sticking out of the monster's neck were in fact the metal electrodes used to electrify the creature during the creation sequence.

Despite Lugosi's contemptuous parting comment – to the effect that the creature was so covered in make-up that the studio might as well get an extra to play him – Whale recognized that the part of the monster needed a very special kind of actor. There are various apocryphal stories about how

Left: An early photograph of Karloff, who spent his first years in Hollywood as a bit-part player.

Below left: Colin Clive as a neurotic Henry Frankenstein, with Dwight Frye as the hunchback, Fritz.

Below: The monster encounters the new Mrs Frankenstein (Mae Clarke), before sweeping her off her feet. . .

Whale 'discovered' Boris Karloff – that he saw him at a restaurant table, or during a screening of the gangster movie *Graft* in which Karloff played a small part as a murderer. Whatever the truth, we know that two things attracted Whale to Karloff. The first was that Karloff's face, with its strong features, heavy-lidded eyes and lugubrious countenance, seemed likely to complement Pierce's make-up. The second was that Karloff's enigmatic personality suited the mixture of pathos and violence that Whale had decided formed the essence of the monster's character.

Karloff, who today is recognized as the classic player of Frankenstein's monster, was born William Henry Pratt in Camberwell, London. His middle-class family had intended him to enter the consular service as a diplomat, but Karloff rebelled and emigrated to Canada. He spent the next ten years working as a laborer and truck driver, and then as an actor in touring companies. He worked in films from 1919, but his roles were minor and the films usually mediocre. In the late 1920s he landed some slightly better supporting roles, but in

1931, at the age of 44, his career must have seemed at something of a dead-end. When Whale offered him the part of Frankenstein's monster, Karloff seized upon it. He later commented on the role, 'It changed my life. I was just another actor until then. It made me a personality.'

Although Karloff remembered 'his monster' with affection, he found the role extremely taxing physically. During shooting his make-up had to be re-applied every morning, and this took between four and six hours. If any of the make-up melted into his eyes it caused excruciating pain, and it was extremely difficult for Karloff to eat properly or to relax until Pierce had scraped away his artistry at the end of the working day. To make matters worse the film was shot during the fiercest part of the Californian summer, and the costume was heavy – 48 pounds – and hot. Karloff sweated so much that he later said it seemed as if he were acting in 'a clammy shroud.'

At the time Karloff was not a star, and anyway hated complaining, so the studio never made any real effort to alleviate his awful working conditions. There is a story that at one point Karloff was taking a short relaxing walk off-set in full make-up, when a secretary suddenly appeared round a corner. The girl screamed and collapsed, and from that moment on the studio ordered Karloff to wear a blue veil over his head at all times when he was off-set. Karloff certainly did wear a veil over his head for much of the shooting, although whether this was because of fainting secretaries, or because the Laemmles were aware that certain kinds of secrecy gave rise to excellent advance publicity, is a moot point.

Undoubtedly the casting of Karloff as the monster provided the most striking visual element in the film. The rest of the cast varied from competent to rather good, but all were overawed by Karloff and Pierce's creation. Colin Clive played the monster's creator (called in the film series Henry, rather than Victor, Frankenstein) as a jumpy neurotic. The script encouraged him to accentuate the 'obsessed scientist' side of Frankenstein's character, rather than the guilt-ridden victim portrayed in the novel. Clive was much admired by his fellow actors but, as a worsening alcoholic who was also rumored to be married to a lesbian, his private life was regarded as tragic. The actor died of consumption in 1938, before the *Frankenstein* series was completed.

Dwight Frye, who ably played the hunchback Fritz, was known to specialize in grotesques and went on to play various other minor roles in the *Frankenstein* series. The role of Elizabeth was acted, a little woodenly, by Mae Clarke, who is perhaps better remembered as the girl whose face Jimmy Cagney smothered in grapefruit in the famous 1931 gangster movie, *Public Enemy*.

Throughout the *Frankenstein* series the set design, lighting and special effects are at least as important as the supporting cast. It is worth pointing out that in the novel there is no mention of romantic castles, marvelous laboratories or picturesque villages. The original Frankenstein is a member of the bourgeoisie rather than the nobility, and much of the action takes place in dramatic natural settings such as Alpine glaciers, lakesides and the wasteland of the Orkneys.

However, Whale knew that his film needed a more contrived form of spectacle. In particular he sensed that the creation sequence in *Frankenstein* was bound to be vital in

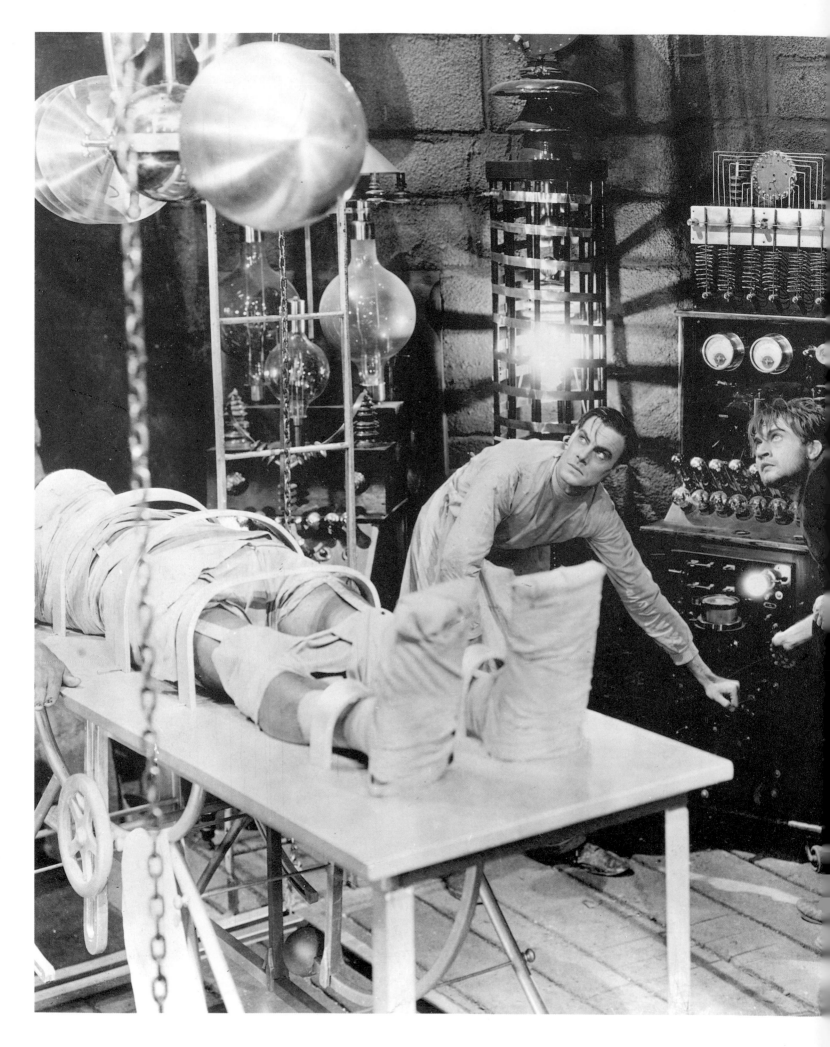

Left: Moving the plot to a modern setting ensured that the special effects department could create a truly terrifying laboratory. The combination of the Gothic tower, lightning, and mysterious twentieth-century scientific equipment made the creation scene spectacular.

Below: Fritz, the hunchback assistant, was another departure from Mary Shelley's text. He was the prototype for a succession of weird assistants to mad scientists in other movies.

grabbing the audience's interest and in persuading them to 'suspend their disbelief'. Abandoning the novel's bare attic room, he set the sequence in a grand Gothic watchtower packed with mysterious scientific equipment. Great machinery hoisted a table plus the monster skywards to the life-giving lightning. Karloff, who was of course strapped half-naked to the table, later commented, 'I could see directly above me the special effects men brandishing the white-hot scissor-like carbons that made the lightning.' This understandably terrified Karloff, but the sequence itself is a tremendous success.

As was previously mentioned, the Frankenstein film is based at least as much on earlier stage versions of the story as it is on the original novel. A large number of the differences between the novel and the film can be explained either by this or by the mechanical need to simplify and abbreviate Mary Shelley's long and complex plot.

Certain other changes are fascinating, however, for the insight they give into the differing priorities of the novelist and film-maker, and because they highlight how very much of what we think of as 'Frankenstein' is formed from the Universal film rather than the original story.

An obvious example is the inclusion in the film of the mad stunted Fritz as assistant to Frankenstein. If at times Fritz appears to have wandered out of a darker version of the Hunchback of Notre Dame, this is probably no coincidence – it was the great success of Universal's Hunchback that prompted the studio towards horror movies in the first place.

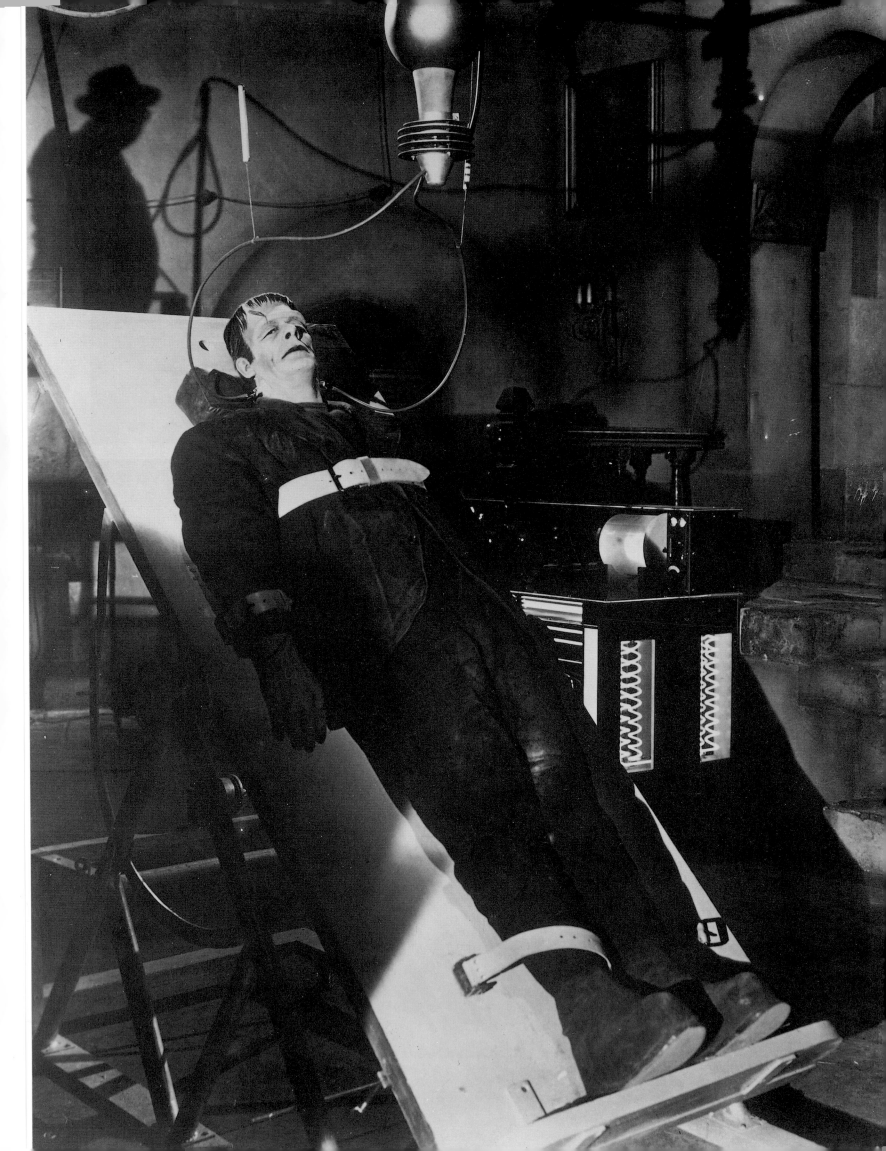

Monster Mania

'Titans of terror, clashing in mortal combat!'

PUBLICITY FOR *Frankenstein Meets The Wolf Man*

Many horror fans believe that *Bride of Frankenstein* (1935), the sequel to the 1931 *Frankenstein*, is even better than the original. Although the basic engine of the plot – that the monster wants a bride – and certain set pieces (such as the blind hermit scenes) are plucked from the novel, James Whale had by now succeeded in unshackling his monster from Mary Shelley, and his strange imagination was able to roam free.

The film opens with a prologue. It is a thundery night in the mountains around Lake Geneva. The famous literary group of Byron, Shelley and Mary Shelley are gathered together. Mary reveals that her saga of *Frankenstein* is not yet finished.

Picking up from the final sequences of *Frankenstein* (1931), the tale begins at the burned out windmill. The vengeful father of little Maria prods the remnants of the structure, hoping to find evidence of the death of his child's killer. The ground gives way, and he falls into the underground reservoir that has allowed the monster to survive. The unlucky man is quickly dispatched.

Meanwhile, the recovering Frankenstein is visited by an evil scientist, Pretorius. Frankenstein visits Pretorius's laboratory, which provides the setting for one of Universal's most lauded special effects scenes – a collection of glass bottles containing tiny 'homunculi' or little humans. Pretorius tries to persuade Frankenstein to resume his experiments.

In a scene derived from the original novel, the wandering monster frightens a girl, who falls into a pond. When he hauls her out, the monster is fired upon by hunters, who assume he is assaulting the child. A mob of villagers now pursue the monster, who rolls boulders down upon them but who is eventually overwhelmed and trussed up. His incarceration in the village is short-lived however, and he resumes his cheerless wanderings. He happens across a blind hermit, and the lonely desperation of the monster in the early stages of Mary Shelley's novel is conjured up in the following scenes, as the monster develops a touching relationship with the old man. In one scene the monster even merrily hiccups over his wine and takes to smoking cigars.

Of course, the monster's happiness is doomed. Hunters arrive and chase him off, the mob resumes its pursuit, and in an act symbolizing his despair the monster topples over the giant statue of a bishop in a ghostly graveyard.

Pretorius and the monster enter into an unholy alliance in order to create a monster-bride. They force Frankenstein to co-operate by kidnapping his wife, Elizabeth. The tower laboratory again resounds to the hum of giant electrical machinery. The bandaged corpse of the Bride is at last made ready, and hoisted to the top of the tower, where giant kites wheel across the sky in order to capture the lightning.

The table is lowered, and the bandages are stripped to reveal a seven-foot Elsa Lanchester, her black hair worked into a massive backward sweeping coiffure, with silver streaks resembling lightning flashing back from her temples. The face of the Bride is frozen and mad, with horrible rosebud lips and angry slanting eyebrows. Yet hers is not the clumsy misshapen ugliness of the original monster, and as he gazes adoringly at her proud face, happy at last to have a companion, the audience begins to guess the tragic outcome.

Longing for her to speak, the monster asks pathetically, 'Friend?' But her only answer is a vicious scream, and it becomes obvious that she will always loathe him. Crashing through the laboratory in a mad rage, the creature shows that

he has forgiven his creator by warning him to leave before he pulls the lever that explodes the whole building – but he insists that the evil Pretorius remain.

Of course, an account of the plot cannot provide an answer to the most interesting question of all: What exactly is it that allows *Bride of Frankenstein* to escape the miserable fate of most horror sequels?

Perhaps the first thing to remember is that Whale was able to assemble much the same talented crew and cast (with the exception of Mae Clarke) as for the original film. His cast had reached the point where the fundamental problems of character definition and make-up had been overcome, and they could look to develop the sequel in new directions.

Whale was not too proud to repeat and remodel certain sequences that had worked well first time round. Thus we have even more impressive laboratory and 'peasant chase' scenes. He recognized, however, that now that the monster had been revealed the film would need some extraordinary new special effects. The marvelous homunculi in Pretorius's laboratory, though hardly necessary to the plot, are the memorable result.

Page 34: In House of Frankenstein, *it was Glenn Strange's turn to receive the life-giving electricity in his electrodes.*

These pages: *Four years after the runaway success of* Frankenstein, Universal *produced* The Bride of Frankenstein *as a sequel to the original. Elsa Lanchester (above) starred as both Mary Shelley and the monster's mate. Spectacular special effects like the small 'homonculi' (far right) helped ensure that box office returns were gratifyingly high.*

Left: *One addition to the cast of* The Bride of Frankenstein *was the evil scientist Pretorius, who persuades Frankenstein to resume his work. Once again, Universal constructed a laboratory full of nightmarish equipment.*

Right: *Boris Karloff with (from left) Basil Rathbone, Lionel Atwill and Bela Lugosi in 1938 on the set of* Son of Frankenstein.

Below: *One of the most poignant images in* Bride of Frankenstein: *the misunderstood monster is caught by a posse of foolish peasants.*

The cinematography, excellent in the first film, is simply superb in Bride of Frankenstein. The camera work is full of bold and unusual shots, with a maximum use of shadow and contrast. The production values throughout the Frankenstein series were (and still are) uniquely high for a horror series, but the Bride of Frankenstein and its sequel, Son of Frankenstein, are particularly outstanding in their ingenuity and opulence. The fantastic sets in Bride of Frankenstein turn the grim wanderings of the monster into a progress through a mythical landscape.

Yet the real power of the film stems from two distinct elements. Firstly, the director indulges his rather bitter sense of humor in some wonderfully macabre scenes, which give the film quite a different tone from the earlier movie. Whale skilfully weaves grotesque tableaux of drunken monsters, furtive grave-robbers, and foolish peasants into the storyline so that they counterbalance his more weighty themes. An interesting example of the latter is the way Whale stresses the misunderstood and suffering nature of the monster by filling certain shots with religious symbolism. When the baying vigilantes truss up the creature, the scene is composed in such a way as to remind the audience of Christ's condemnation by the mob and His eventual crucifixion.

The second reason the film has such a powerful impact can be simply stated: Boris Karloff. Despite the demands of a daily make-up ordeal that extended in this sequel to five hours, and the fact that an antagonistic Whale refused to accept his views on characterization, Karloff gave the finest performance of his career. He quite correctly warned Whale that it was a dangerous move artistically to allow the monster to speak. But when Whale insisted, Karloff turned the fault to advantage, using the stilted dialogue to emphasize even more effectively than in his original wholly mimed performance how the creature longs for true communication and human contact. His final line, bellowed to his ghastly Bride in a tone of self-horror and loathing, reveals the monster's dreadful acceptance of his fate: 'We belong dead.'

Although *Bride of Frankenstein* was greatly praised by the critics, and proved to be a major commercial success, it could easily have been the last *Frankenstein* movie made by Universal. By 1936 the studio was in deep financial crisis. The Laemmles were forced to grant an option to buy their business to the Standard Capital Corporation in return for a loan. The sharks closed in, and eventually old Carl Laemmle Sr. was forced to hand over his studio to the SCC. At the age of 28, Laemmle Jr. retired to a mansion and never worked again.

The new regime was distinctly hostile to horror films, which it regarded as morally dubious and financially risky. However, in 1938 it came to the studio's notice that a Los Angeles theater was doing extraordinary business showing a horror triple bill that included the original *Frankenstein*. They rushed out a billing of *Dracula* and *Frankenstein*, and prepared to produce a new *Frankenstein* sequel.

This third film in the Hollywood series, *Son of Frankenstein* (1939), manages to introduce an American family into its plot. It opens with Wolf von Frankenstein, his wife Elsa and their son Peter emigrating from their home in the States to begin a new life at the castle of Wolf's infamous father in MittelEurope. The local villagers give the family a hostile reception, and an early visitor to the castle is the local police chief, Krogh, who when he was a child had his arm torn out of its socket by the monster.

As Wolf tours his father's decaying laboratory, Ygor introduces himself. Exhibiting a black sense of humor, Ygor explains that he got his horribly misshapen neck when he was hung for stealing bodies. In the intervening time, Ygor has used the monster to revenge himself upon the jurors who condemned him. But now the monster lies unconscious after having been hit by lightning.

Wolf manages to revive the monster, who is immediately instructed by Ygor to finish off the remaining jurors. Accused by the police chief of resuming his father's awful experiments, Wolf attempts to exile Ygor from the estate. Ygor attacks him with a hammer, and is shot dead.

Right: Elsa Lanchester's make-up
as the monster's mate was
masterly. The dramatic silver
streaks in her hair, and the elegant
bandage gown, produced a
monster unlike any other.

CARL LAEMMLE Presents   THE MON

THE BRIDE

After discovering the body of his friend Ygor, the monster revenges himself by kidnapping Wolf's little boy, Peter. He intends to hurl the child into a lake of boiling sulphur, but Peter is so friendly and trusting towards him that he cannot bring himself to do it before Wolf, his wife and the police chief arrive at the lake in hot pursuit. In the ensuing battle, the monster tears off Krogh's wooden arm, but, Wolf swings down on a chain and kicks the monster into the sulphur lake. Wolf and his family finally renounce their estate, and return to America.

While the first two *Frankenstein* films are recognized as classics in their own right, the later Universal films have a standing only as a part of a classic series. Many horror fans would argue that *Son of Frankenstein* also deserves individual classic status, but although it is a very fine film it somehow lacks the epic feeling of its predecessors.

Apart from the departure of the Laemmles as producers, there were other major changes in the *Frankenstein* team. James Whale's career had gone into terminal decline, and the tragic Colin Clive had died of consumption. Karloff played the monster one last time, but his heart was not really in it. Even

before shooting started he had decided that the script reduced his monster to a lumbering giant. He was right; only in the final scenes is the monster called upon to do any real terrorizing. Karloff had too much affection for his monster simply to churn films out, and he vowed never to play the part again.

However, there were great strengths in the rest of the cast. Basil Rathbone, playing Wolf von Frankenstein, was at the peak of his powers and excelled at portraying handsome and urbane villains. Rathbone and Lionel Atwill, who played the suspicious police chief, Krogh, enter into some entertaining verbal sparring. Atwill, a noted eccentric in his private life who used to enjoy attending murder trials and organizing sordid Hollywood parties, amused himself by developing various idiosyncrasies for his character. Perhaps the most memorable is Krogh's habit of sticking darts into his wooden arm in between rounds of the game.

The most inspired piece of casting was to pick old Bela Lugosi to play Ygor. Lugosi, whose career was on the rocks, fell upon the role joyously. He cast aside his previous vanity and took a wicked delight in the crook-necked appearance

Left: Dracula *and*
Frankenstein *were obvious
partners for a double-bill, both
apparently encouraging hysterical
audience reactions.*

Right and below: *Boris Karloff
played the monster for the last time
in 1939 in* Son of
Frankenstein. *Basil Rathbone
played Wolf von Frankenstein, an
American who emigrated to his
father's European castle and
managed to revive his father's
monster. The monster kidnaps
Wolf's son as revenge when he
discovers the body of his friend
Ygor (a part played with relish by
Bela Lugosi).*

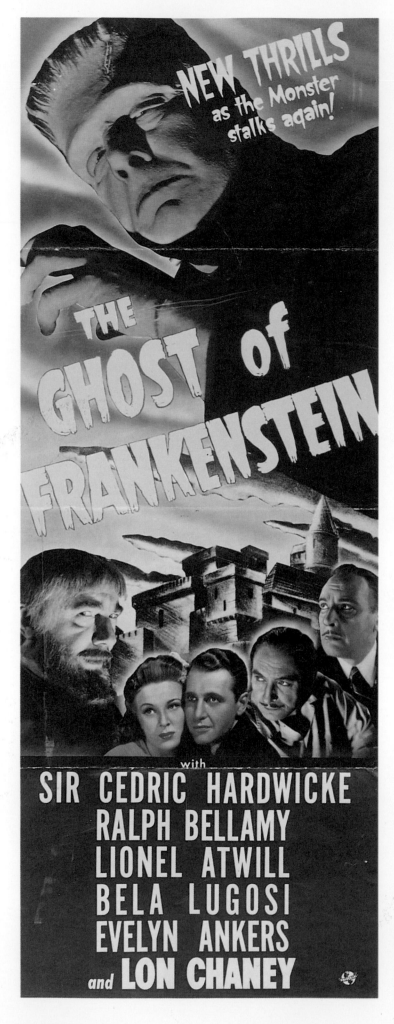

Jack Pierce devised for him. Free to act the sinister fool, he capers around his friend, the monster, and succeeds in stealing the show.

Apart from the casting, the major contribution of new director Rowland V Lee was to insist on high production values. Although *Son of Frankenstein* lacks the haunting strangeness of the two earlier films, its sets and lighting are still remarkable. Unlike the later films in the series, one can reproduce almost any still knowing that it will appear to be a work of art in its own right.

The Ghost of Frankenstein (1941) is really the first of the production-line Frankensteins. Universal were still prepared to fund above-average production values and to organize a decent cast, but the novelty and excitement of the first three films are largely lacking.

The rather tortuous plot begins with Ygor annoying the local villagers by playing his horn loudly at night from the top of the Frankenstein castle tower. When the local villagers try to destroy the castle, Ygor discovers the monster encased in hardened sulphur (presumably deposited from the sulphur lake the creature plunged into at the end of the previous film).

The monster breaks free, and the ghastly pair journey to the village of Vasaria, where the grandson of the original Baron Frankenstein is now working as a brilliant surgeon. After various episodes that are often re-workings of sequences in the earlier films (for example, the monster helps a little girl retrieve her ball from a roof, but is set upon by a mob of villagers . . .), the film climaxes in an extended brain-swapping routine.

This finale is an excellent example of the quirky mixture of horror and humor that make even the lesser Frankenstein movies so watchable half a century after they were made. During it, the monster wants his own brain to be replaced with that of the little girl; Frankenstein wants to replace the monster's brain with that of his murdered assistant; and Ygor wants to put his own brain in the monster's body so that he can go around terrorizing people.

Ygor gets his way, but goes blind immediately because his blood-type is wrong. The maddened monster-Ygor then hurls himself around the laboratory, causing the usual climactic mayhem and destruction.

Sadly, the weakest aspect of the film is the monster itself. With the departure of Karloff, Universal were forced to cast around for a suitable replacement. They chose Lon Chaney Jr, who in 1941 had scored his first great success with Universal's *The Wolf Man*. Although Jack Pierce had created Chaney's Wolf Man make-up, their relationship on the set of *Ghost of Frankenstein* was unhappy. None of the Frankenstein 'old hands' considered Chaney as professional as Karloff, and the director soon realized that if he did not get most of the shooting over by the afternoon he was in danger of getting a monster with slurred speech and unsteady legs.

None of this would have mattered on-screen if Chaney had been able to invest the role with any real emotion. Unfortunately, while he was able to rampage well enough, Chaney never succeeded in animating the monster's face. When watching the film it is impossible not to feel nostalgic for Karloff's tragic eyes and expressive hands.

THE PHANTOM MONSTER SHOW!

HORROR HIT No. 1

HORROR HIT No. 2

Basil RATHBONE • Boris KARLOFF • Bela LUGOSI in

SON OF FRANKENSTEIN "the Bride of FRANKENSTEIN

Above and right: Universal discovered early on that horror movies were instant money spinners. Showing them as double-bills guaranteed large box-office receipts, as did employing all the public's favorite monsters in one film: House of Frankenstein (right).

Left: Lon Chaney Jnr. stalked the screen as the monster in The Ghost of Frankenstein.

THE HOUSE OF FRANKENSTEIN

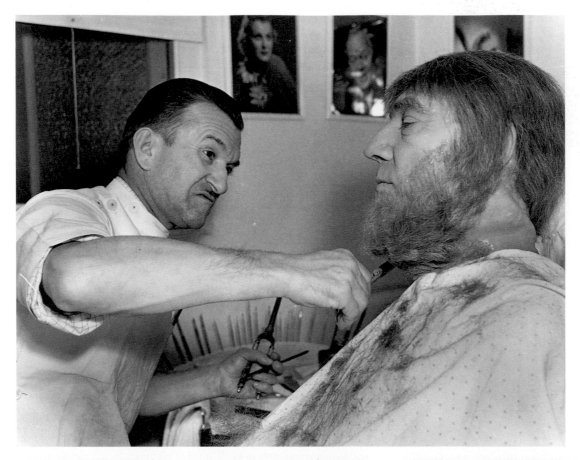

Left: Jack Pierce transforms Bela Lugosi into the wicked, capering Ygor of Son of Frankenstein. A former stuntman and character actor, Pierce enjoyed a varied career on both sides of the camera, but really found his niche as head of the make-up department at Universal Studios.

Below left: Ygor retrieves a sulphur-encrusted monster from a castle dungeon at the beginning of The Ghost of Frankenstein.

Below: Wolf von Frankenstein and Police Chief Krogh eye each other suspiciously over the tea-table in Son of Frankenstein. Lionel Atwill took to the role of the embittered one-armed police chief with relish, amusing both audiences and cast members by sticking darts in his wooden arm.

Right: Lon Chaney Jr. plays the traditional game of snatching a small child in order to enliven a plodding plot in The Ghost of Frankenstein. He was really interested in her mind, however, and was keen to try out her brain for himself.

931-70

48

Left: Having survived immersion in a sulphur pit, and a head-to-head session with Ygor when they exchanged brains, the monster finally goes out in a blaze of glory. Lon Chaney Jr. in The Ghost of Frankenstein.

Right and below: By the 1940s, Universal realized that audiences were not satisfied with just one monster per film, and began to fill their horror movies with legions of sinister stars.

Luckily the monster again had a strong supporting cast. Sir Cedric Hardwicke, a noted English stage actor, brought a certain aplomb to his role as Frankenstein the surgeon, while Bela Lugosi repeated his wonderfully horrible Ygor. Jack Otterson, who was also the designer for *Son of Frankenstein*, produced some excellent sets, so that some of the scenes, such as the opening attack on the castle by the peasants, are up to classic standards.

Given that Universal had created both the cinematic Frankenstein's monster and the Wolf Man, it was perhaps inevitable that the studio would try to bring both characters together. Lon Chaney Jr. had played both roles and there was even some talk of him playing both monsters at once in *Frankenstein Meets the Wolf Man* (1943). However, the idea was eventually dropped because of the practical difficulties.

Instead, the studio asked Bela Lugosi to fill the role that he had turned down so contemptuously over ten years before, when the first *Frankenstein* was cast. Unfortunately by now Lugosi was over 60 and in no condition to endure the physical demands of the part. Without the happy substitution of a stunt man (Eddie Parker) in several major scenes and most action sequences, the film would not have been finished on schedule. Lugosi was fighting a losing battle anyway. His face is simply the wrong shape to complement Jack Pierce's make-up.

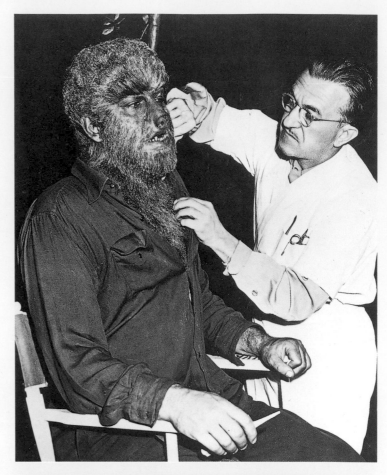

In addition, the studio's original decision to give the monster dialogue wrecked whatever credibility Lugosi might have been able to build up. When the completed film was first viewed by studio executives the showing was interrupted by hysterical laughter every time the monster spoke. A monster with a thick Hungarian accent just did not seem credible!

As a result all the monster's dialogue was cut from the released film. This was probably a wise decision – except that the film editors forgot that it was the monster himself who explained to the Wolf Man that in this film the monster is blind. Thus, to anyone who forgets the final sequence in *Ghost of Frankenstein*, Lugosi's stumbling, groping giant suggests that either the actor spent his lunch-hours trying to drink Lon Chaney under the table, or that every page of his script had been accidentally stamped MIDNIGHT.

The meandering script was written by Curt Siodmak, one of Universal's top writers, who had also devised the original *Wolf Man* script. Understandably, therefore, it has a lycanthropic bias. In this film Frankenstein's monster is just a monster, and it is really the hairy Lon Chaney who plays the tragic and dominant role.

Despite all this, *Frankenstein Meets the Wolf Man* has a special place in the hearts of all Frankenstein fans. It has some wonderful set pieces, especially the joyful village scenes during the 'Festival of the New Wine.' But, most of all, the relationship between the monster and the Wolf Man is delightfully bizarre, and their final battle is truly thrilling.

After the healthy, if not outstanding, financial success of *Frankenstein Meets the Wolf Man*, Universal were tempted into producing two movies that contained all their stock horror characters.

The studio must have realized that the currency of each individual monster would be devalued. However, it seems that they suspected this was happening anyway and that the jaded

These pages: In 1943, Bela Lugosi added another character to his horror portfolio, and stretched Jack Pierce's artistry still further by becoming the monster in Frankenstein Meets the Wolf Man. Lugosi was not an altogether natural choice for the role; his voice in particular was ridiculed by preview audiences who were simply not scared by a monster with a Hungarian accent. Lon Chaney Jr. played the wolfman, alternating between a pensive, clean-shaven hero and a horrifying hirsute hooligan.

51

audience would be wowed by the idea of 'monster parties'. After all, what could be more appetizing to a horror fan than a goulash of Frankenstein's monster, the Wolf Man, and Dracula, spiced up with the usual gypsies, mad scientists, hunchbacks and 'MittelEuropean' sets? After watching the films, horror fans might well retort, 'A decent, original script.'

In the first film, *The House of Frankenstein* (1944), Boris Karloff returned to the series to play the 'mad scientist' role. His character, imprisoned for transplanting a man's brain into a dog, breaks out of jail with a hunchback (brilliantly played by J. Carrol Naish, who almost repeats Bela Lugosi's feat in earlier films of stealing the film from under the monster's nose).

The dreadful duo trundle around MittelEurope in a hijacked carnival wagon – 'Professor Lampini's Chamber of Horrors.' The first part of the film is dominated by Dracula, whose bones formed part of Professor Lampini's exhibition. Dracula is destroyed after a dramatic coach chase, and the Karloff character then defrosts the Wolf Man and the monster from an ice cavern. Romantic interest is added in the form of a gypsy, who falls in love with Wolf Man but is eventually obliged to shoot him dead with a silver bullet.

During all this the monster, played by newcomer Glenn Strange, does very little except lie strapped to a table looking threatening. Eventually the creature is given his usual fix of a few thousand megavolts and comes as near to life as the limited acting talents of Strange could manage. Karloff, always the gentleman, offered Strange much good advice on playing the part, but he must have sensed that Strange's charisma level was more suited to a bit-part in zombie movies than to the greatest horror role of them all.

But perhaps this is too hard. Strange does well enough in the action sequences, and at this stage in the series that is really the most one can hope for. By now the monster was no longer one of Universal's most prized possessions; it had been reduced to a tired old thing that would simply be worn out in as financially effective a way as possible.

The plot for the last 'monster party', *House of Dracula* (1945), manages to be both bizarre and derivative. It revolves around Onslow Stevens's wonderfully hammy mad scientist (this time with a *female* hunchback assistant), bone-softening plants, and an entertaining Dracula who begs to be cured of his 'blood disease.'

Lon Chaney Jr. turns in another unmemorable performance as the Wolf Man, while the plot and Glenn Strange conspire to leave the monster catatonic for most of the movie.

By the end of the film the Wolf Man has been cured of his lycanthropy, and in the finale he is free to escape from the fiery chaos of the laboratory. The monster is left to perish alone and, in a sense, forever.

Above and left: House of Frankenstein, *released in 1944, provided horror fans with all their favorite fiends together in one movie. With Boris Karloff as the evil Professor Lampini, Dracula, the Wolf Man and Frankenstein's monster all capered through 'MittelEurope', terrifying the simple peasants.*

Right: House of Dracula (1945), *exploited the same 'monster ensemble' idea. Onslow Stevens played the mad scientist, while Glenn Strange, as the monster, plodded through a film that bore very little relation to the original stories of either* Frankenstein *or* Dracula.

Frankenstein gets Hammered

'. . . now that I had finished, the beauty

of the dream vanished and breathless horror and

disgust filled my heart.'

MARY SHELLEY, *Frankenstein*

Hollywood's Frankenstein monster was laid to rest in the *House of Dracula*, but in the 1960s a transformed version of the character was revived in the emerging British horror film laboratory. Just as the Hollywood *Frankenstein* is associated with Universal and the 1930s, so this transatlantic monster is redolent of Hammer Films and the 'swinging sixties'.

Hammer Films was created out of an earlier film company in 1947. Their first productions tended to be sleuth movies such as *Cloudburst* (1951), which like many Hammer films starred an American lead (Robert Preston) to make it more palatable to an American audience.

Hammer's first venture into science fiction was *Four-Sided Triangle* (1953), in which a love-struck scientist designs a machine that can duplicate the girl who has just jilted him. However, the early production that every horror fan remembers is *The Quatermass Experiment* (1955), the classic tale of how a spaceman returns to earth only to be gradually taken over by an alien force within him. Richard Wordsworth's performance as the deranged astronaut is one of the most haunting in the science fiction film genre.

In 1957 Hammer launched themselves into period horror with a minor classic – *The Curse of Frankenstein*. It is difficult to imagine a more abrupt departure from the old Hollywood formula. Whereas the Universal films were shot in an elegant, lavishly produced black and white, this Hammer film set the tone for the rest of the Hammer series by making the most of lurid color and a shoe-string budget. The Hammer script writers returned to the Mary Shelley novel to gain inspiration, but like Robert Florey before them they decided to interpret the work loosely. The studio's make-up artists might well

have allowed themselves to be influenced by Jack Pierce's conception of the monster, except that Universal had carefully copyrighted his creation.

This is perhaps lucky for horror fans, as the Hammer monster is entirely fresh. It is true that with its glaring eye and mess of scar tissue Christopher Lee's creature looks more like an acid-burn victim than a being sewn together, but this is surely better than an inferior version of Boris Karloff.

In *The Curse of Frankenstein* Peter Cushing, as Frankenstein, murders a brilliant scientist in order to implant his brain in his monster. When Frankenstein's assistant objects to this a struggle ensues, and the brain is damaged. In this way, Hammer repeated the 'damaged brain' detail of the original Universal script without actually copying the Universal plot. The monster's damaged brain leads him to cause a predictable amount of murder and mayhem, and in the finale, as a form of rough justice, Frankenstein himself is condemned to death by guillotine for his creature's misdoings.

The *Curse of Frankenstein* proved to be a great financial success for Hammer, both in Britain and the United States. Like Universal before them, Hammer had chanced upon the rich vein of horror, and they were not going to let the genre escape easily. Indeed, they simply followed Universal in reverse and announced that their next horror billing would be *Dracula* (1958). Eventually Hammer produced six *Frankenstein* movies, each tending to be more gory and bizarre in storyline than the last.

In the *The Revenge of Frankenstein* (1958) Peter Cushing repeated his measured performance as the obsessed scientist. It is noticeable that whereas in the 1930s Colin Clive played Frankenstein as a neurotic, Peter Cushing's character is cool

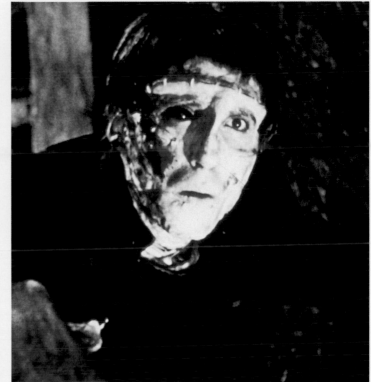

Page 54: In 1957 Frankenstein's monster changed shape once more, as Christopher Lee took up the part in The Curse of Frankenstein.

Above: The Curse of Frankenstein starred Peter Cushing as Frankenstein, and Christopher Lee as a scar-ridden monster. This film moved nearer to Mary Shelley's original plot, and made full use of color, by dwelling on the more gory aspects of the story.

Right: Peter Cushing returned to play the misguided Baron in The Revenge of Frankenstein in 1958.

Left: The Horror of Frankenstein (1970) produced yet another variation on the monster's appearance. Dave Prowse chilled audiences with his portrayal of the axe-wielding outcast.

and calculating. In this way the Hammer films moved away from the romantic image of the scientist carried away by his vision, which so dominates the original novel, towards the sixties' conception of the scientist as a dangerous cynic beyond the control of society.

Cushing, who entered into the role of Frankenstein with much enthusiasm, even took to visiting museums to see and handle old surgical instruments. He relates in his memoirs that his portrayal of Frankenstein in the later part of the Hammer series was much affected by a film he made in 1959 called *The Flesh and the Fiends.* In this he played Dr Robert Knox, a celebrated Scottish anatomist, who was eventually forced to flee Edinburgh after it became clear that corpses he had dissected had been procured by the infamous body-stealers, Burke and Hare. Of course Burke and Hare, who made a living by enticing the unwary into their lodging house in order to suffocate them and sell their bodies to Knox, were the inspiration behind the body-stealing characters that appear so commonly in the Hammer and Universal versions of the *Frankenstein* story.

Returning to *The Revenge of Frankenstein,* we find the Baron undeterred by a close encounter with the guillotine that one assumed had cut off his head at the end of the first film. He starts experimenting again, and this time he succeeds in creating a sane monster. Unfortunately, after the creature is brain-damaged during a violent struggle, it develops a hunger for human flesh and embarks on a series of murderous sprees.

The Hammer scripts had by now developed as entities independent of either the original novel or their Universal predecessors. Unfortunately for horror fans, the Hammer plots were largely independent of each other as well. The Universal series contains some notorious discrepancies, but it can still be viewed as one long story. This is certainly not the case with the Hammer films, and it is rather pointless to try to view them consecutively.

Of course, it would be wrong to imply that the Hammer films were uninfluenced by the Universal versions, even though the director of much of the Hammer series, Terence Fisher, insisted that they should be viewed entirely separately. For example, the third Hammer film, *The Evil of Frankenstein*, opens with a derivative scene of outraged peasants chasing the scientist Frankenstein. Of course, even here there is a subtle difference, for in the famous 1930s 'peasant chase' scenes the fugitive was always the monster, not his creator. This highlights a major change of focus between the Hollywood and Hammer series, for in the latter the monster always

plays second bill to the evil scientist, and sometimes does not even appear at all.

The third film in Hammer's *Frankenstein* series, *The Evil of Frankenstein*, was made in 1964. It is a rather baroque tale of how Frankenstein rediscovers his monster frozen in a cavern, but finds that the only person who can control him is a sinister hypnotist called the Great Zoltan. Zoltan sends the monster off on various immoral errands until the creature rebels and drives a spear through him. Hammer was well aware that its audience demanded romantic interest, and in this film it is provided by a beautiful deaf and dumb girl.

Hammer could not resist bringing the sexual element to the fore in their next tale – *Frankenstein Created Woman* (1966). Like the later Universal films, the plot revolves around the

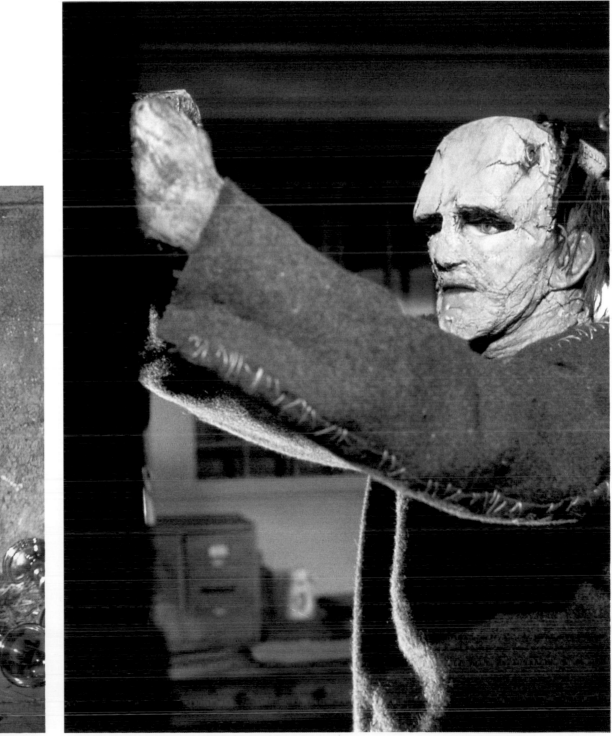

idea of brain swaps. When Frankenstein's assistant is beheaded for a crime he did not commit, and his lover, a deformed girl called Christina, drowns herself, Frankenstein decides to transfer the assistant's brain to Christina's body. At the same time he gives Christina a perfect body, so that she emerges from the bandages with hardly a stitch on her – in both senses of the phrase.

Christina is undoubtedly the sexiest monster ever created, but her creator soon discovers that beauty counts for little if it comes with a warped brain. Christina's only passion is a homicidal urge to avenge her executed lover; when her mission is completed she leaps to her death from a great cliff.

Although *Frankenstein Must Be Destroyed* (1969) does not really have a proper monster, many fans regard it as the nastiest film in the Hammer series. This is largely on account of the high gore-score, which includes a lovely scene of Frankenstein grinding his way through a skull using only the most primitive of hand-drills. But it is also because of the thick vein of psychological unpleasantness that runs through the plot. There are few sympathetic characters, and Frankenstein succeeds in stealing the brain of a deranged genius and installing it in a new body by blackmailing and manipulating all those around him.

The Horror of Frankenstein (1970) returns to the original *Frankenstein* themes, and is really a remake of the first Hammer movie, *The Curse of Frankenstein*. In this instance Ralph Bates, who is competent but lacks the chilling presence of Peter Cushing, plays the mad Baron, while Dave Prowse (now well

known for his part as Darth Vader in *Star Wars*) takes over Christopher Lee's role as the monster. The monster is killed in quite an unusual way: he takes refuge in a barrel when the forces of law and order search the Baron's laboratory, and a child accidentally dowses him with a lethal dose of acid.

The final episode in the Hammer series is perhaps one of the oddest *Frankenstein* movies, and surely has the most lurid title – *Frankenstein and the Monster From Hell* (1973). In this film Frankenstein has used blackmail to gain control of a lunatic asylum. In his secret laboratory within the asylum grounds he has assembled a massive, hairy ape-like monster from the parts of dead patients. Because his hands were so badly burnt in a previous film, all the stitching on the monster was carried out by a mute girl known as Angel, who is much loved by both the monster and the other inmates.

A typically tasteless part of the plot is the explanation of Angel's disability – that she lost her power of speech after being sexually assaulted by the official director of the asylum (who happens to be her father) when she was a child. Never inclined to do things by halves, the Hammer script-writers also introduced the charming plot detail that Frankenstein intends to mate Angel with his ape-beast. Luckily the hapless ape-beast is more excited by the idea of killing the director (of the asylum, sadly, not the film) as a way of revenging his adored Angel. He does this with some style, but is then ripped apart by the other inmates, who mistake his honorable intentions towards the girl.

While Hammer Films were the most consistent exploiters

Left: *Peter Cushing strikes an uncharacteristic pose in* Frankenstein Created Woman *(1967). This film was noteworthy mainly for the beauty of Frankenstein's creation. The film's monster departed from the tradition of a lumbering male bedecked with electrodes, using instead a young woman who shared only a warped brain with previous monsters.*

Right: *In* Frankenstein Must Be Destroyed *(1969), the Baron's ingenuity remains undimmed, with Peter Cushing transplanting the brain of a colleague into another body.*

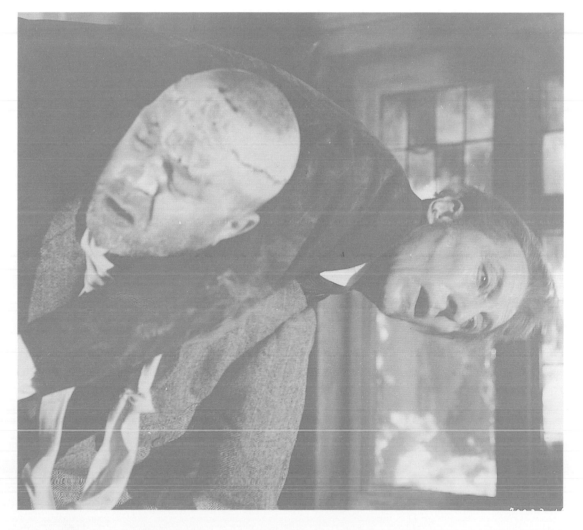

Previous pages: The Horror of Frankenstein (1970) *featured Ralph Bates as the mad baron, and Hammer created a laboratory full of equipment whose very antiquity was chilling.*

Left: Susan Denberg *made an unlikely monster in* Frankenstein Created Woman.

Below and right: Hammer *decided to treat* The Horror of Frankenstein *as a black comedy. Victor Frankenstein (Ralph Bates) finds that he has to murder a few acquaintances in the interests of science. As usual, he is successful at first, but eventually he and his monstrous sidekick (Dave Prowse) meet a nasty end.*

Above: Peter Cushing leaves
Christopher Lee hanging around
while he contemplates his next
hideous experiment.

Left: Zandar Vortov as
Frankenstein's opponent in
Dracula vs Frankenstein.

Right: One of the more bizarre
monster struggles of the cinema:
Furankenshutain tai Baragon,
a Japanese movie made in 1974.

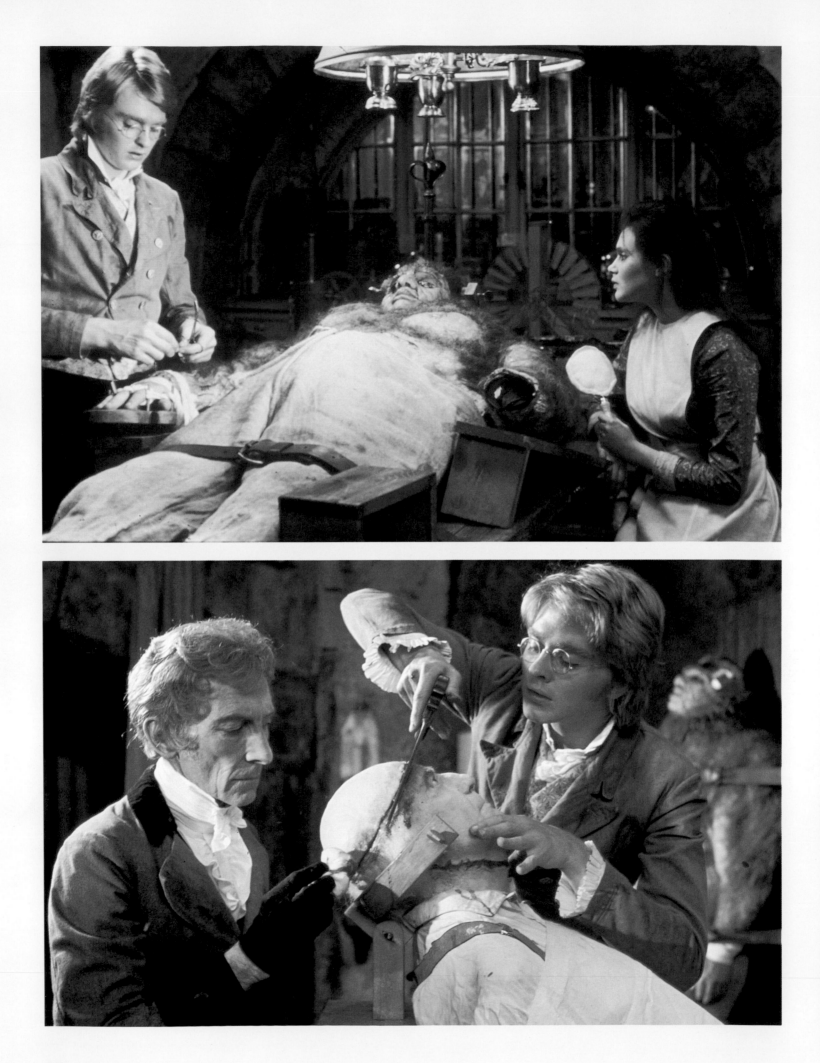

These pages: Frankenstein and the Monster from Hell (1973) was the last of the Hammer Frankenstein movies. The Baron (Peter Cushing, above) blackmails his way into a lunatic asylum and uses the laboratory to turn an injured lunatic into a grotesque apeman. With a fairly tasteless storyline and some ghoulish scenes, this was not a 'classic' Frankenstein movie.

Left: Jesse James meets Frankenstein's Daughter (1966) *took the monster theme and exploited it for all it was worth. Frankenstein's children spend their days practising brain transplants in Mexico, creating a monster that somehow becomes entangled with Jesse James. The monster (played by Cal Bolder) is shot, Jesse goes to prison, and Frankenstein's daughter, in a display of finer feeling that has hitherto been carefully concealed by her family, vows to wait for him until he has served his jail sentence.*

Above: *Dr Charles Frankenstein (Sting) is assisted by Quentin Crisp as he gives life to the perfect woman in* The Bride (1988).

Of course, very often the name Frankenstein and the basic idea of a 'monster man' were all that were borrowed from the original concept. The Japanese *Furankenshutain tai Baragon* (1974) is an example of this, for it simply uses Frankenstein as an off-the-peg monster and arranges an epic fight between him and the 'Baragon' dinosaur monster. The film has its moments, but can only really be recommended to Godzilla fans in search of variety.

Dracula vs. Frankenstein (1971) also stages an epic monster duel, but this is a much less innocent offering. Indeed it is in many respects the most tasteless *Frankenstein* movie ever made (which is something of a feat in itself). The plot is hardly worth detailing; suffice it to say that the monster is revived by Count Dracula and Dr Frankenstein, but he soon falls out with his bloodsucking benefactor over a pretty girl. This leads to a struggle that is entertaining in a rather disgusting sort of a way, with Dracula dispatching his foe by wrenching off both his arms and then his head. But the most distasteful element of this wretched film is the pathetic re-appearances in supporting roles of a corpulent Lon Chaney Jr. and a crippled J. Carrol Naish. Both men were ageing, ill and out of work at the time – which gives them an excuse not open to the director.

of the *Frankenstein* myth during the 1960s and early 1970s, the British studio was hardly alone. 'Frankomania' had spread all over the world, and just as in the early nineteenth century a mass of cheap vaudeville stage productions was spawned by the novel, so in the 1960s the power and strangeness of the *Frankenstein* story was used to energize a clutch of low budgets and lackluster directors.

SEE LOVE-STARVED CREATURES FROM ANOTHER GALAXY!

SEE THE INVASION OF THE WILD BEACH PARTY!

SEE A MAN TURNED INTO A SCREAMING MONSTER!

Alan V. Iselin presents

FRANKENSTEIN MEETS THE SPACE MONSTER

Above: Invaders from outer space battled it out with home-made monsters in the schlock-horror Frankenstein Meets the Space Monster, (1966).

Left: Frankenhooker told the bizarre and touching tale of how a female monster is assembled from the limbs of murdered prostitutes. The monster eventually turns the tables on her creator by giving him an impromptu sex change while he's sleeping!

72

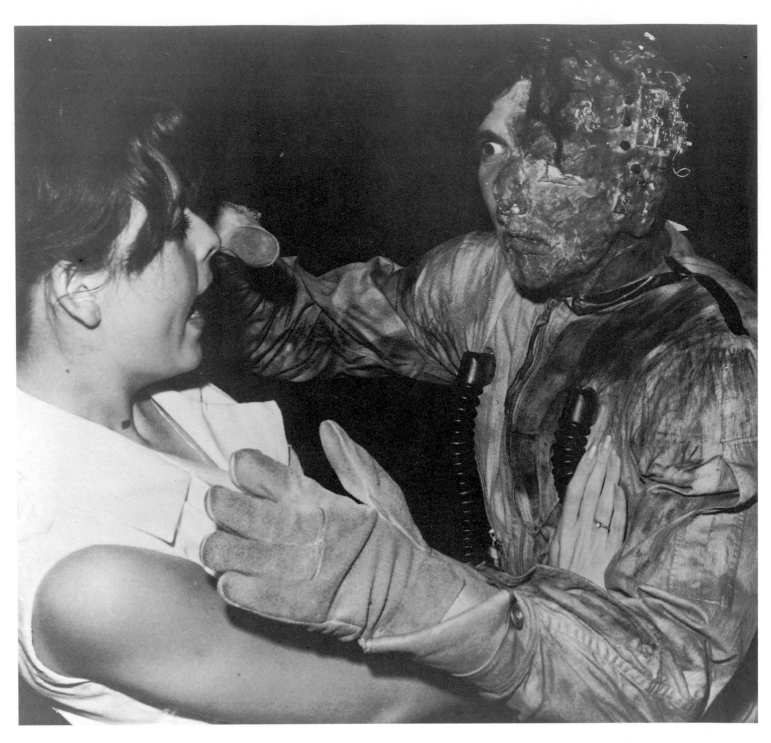

It is worth mentioning in passing the Frankenstein film with the silliest title – *Jesse James Meets Frankenstein's Daughter* (1966). However, even Frankenstein fanatics should be warned that the title comprises at least 90 percent of the film's entertainment value.

One of the wackiest Frankensteins of the period is *Flesh for Frankenstein* (1974), a Franco-Italian production by Andy Warhol. This uses the same theme of black sexual farce as *The Rocky Horror Picture Show*, though not as amusingly. As a Frankenstein film it is pretty mediocre, but it's still a lot more entertaining than *Chelsea Girls*.

By the mid-1960s, then, the Frankenstein monster had been transported to all the most unlikely places on earth, from the B-movies of Japan and the dusty cinemas of Mexico to the innermost recesses of Andy Warhol's imagination. The monster had fought the dreaded Baragon dinosaur and had even

Above: *The Space Monster grapples with an innocent bystander in* Frankenstein Meets the Space Monster.

Right: *Beautiful, but only from the neck up. The monster in* Frankenhooker *shows off her operation scars.*

used a laser gun to save the planet Earth from aliens (*Franken-stein Meets the Spacemonster*, 1966).

And yet one final frontier awaited him. For during the late 1960s and the 1970s the monster was destined to become a porn star. This is not the place to detail the acrobatic talents of the monster lover. It is enough perhaps to say that in such epics as *Les expériences érotiques de Frankenstein* (1972) and *Fanny Hill Meets Dr Erotico* (1968) the creature does so many curious and surprising things that one is left wondering whether he could ever be happy again hurling boulders at peasants and creating simple mayhem. The most recent addition to this sub-genre is the 'splatter' film *Frankenhooker* (1990), which details how a mad scientist obtains body parts by feeding New York tarts an explosive 'supercrack.'

However, not all the recent Frankenstein films have their tongues thrust so firmly in their cheeks. If anything, the most famous post-Hammer movie veers too far in the opposite direction. *Frankenstein: The True Story* (1973) was a Universal NBC production made in England with a largely English cast. Although the film's title is irritatingly misleading, as in many ways the film departs radically from the original story, the production was refreshingly ambitious and well-funded. The plot adds an interesting twist to the tale by allowing the monster to be created beautiful; it is only after some time that the creature starts to suffer from an awful process of physical deterioration that drives him to despair and vengeance. This twist gives the film an interesting psychological angle suggestive of Oscar Wilde's *The Picture of Dorian Gray*.

Although *Frankenstein: The True Story* does suffer from a certain ponderousness, and is overlong at three hours, these faults are redeemed by the excellent design and high production values. Few viewers forget the dreadful scene in which the decomposing creature enters a vast ballroom and walks purposefully over to his scornful Bride, played by the lovely Jane Seymour, only to wrench her head off and cast it at the feet of scientist James Mason. Wonderful stuff!

Above and right:
Frankenstein: The True Story
was a four-hour epic made for TV
by NBC. It was co-authored by
Christopher Isherwood in 1973,
who managed to give the story a
few new twists even after 60 years
of Frankenstein movies. It is one
of the few films to follow the
original novel in setting its
spectacular finale near the North
Pole.

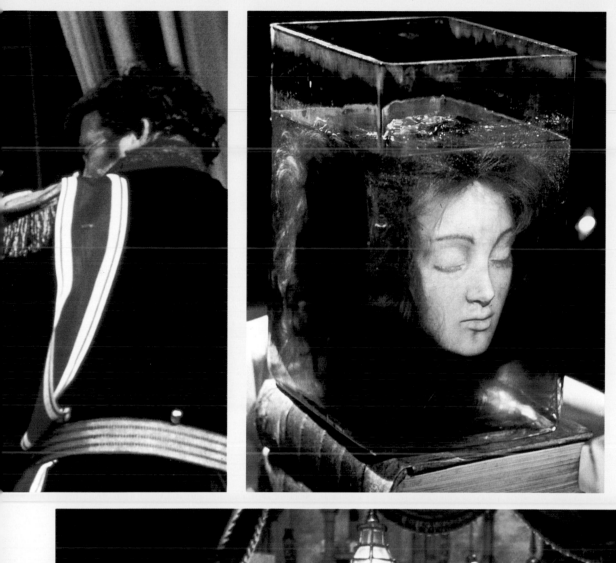

Left and below: One of the radical departures in Frankenstein: The True Story was that the monster began life as a beautiful being. However, he begins to decompose and it is this that drives him to despair. He becomes so bitter that he feels forced to rip off the head of his lovely bride (Jane Seymour, below far left and left).

Funny Frankensteins

'Come up to the lab, and see what's on the slab . . .'

THE ROCKY HORROR PICTURE SHOW

The first notable comedy inspired by the Universal series was the wildly successful Broadway production of *Arsenic and Old Lace* (1941-2). The plot has only a tangential relationship to the *Frankenstein* films: one of the main characters, Jonathan Brewster, has ended up looking like Frankenstein's monster after his partner and plastic surgeon got drunk and watched the famous horror film before operating on him. But this character was acted on Broadway by Boris Karloff himself, and thus the production can be counted as a *Frankenstein* spin-off.

Ironically Karloff's success in the play helped to give him the confidence to turn down the monster part in the later *Frankenstein* films. However, he was unavailable for the classic Hollywood film of the play, and thus most people nowadays associate the role with Raymond Massey.

Abbot and Costello Meet Frankenstein (1948) provided a more direct comic continuation of the classic series, in that it was actually made by Universal. The monster plays second fiddle to the two comics, but given the chance he makes an excellent straight man, especially in the famous scene in which Lou Costello as Wilbur ends up accidentally sitting on the monster's lap and getting his hands mixed up with the creature's giant paws. Costello did not at first think that this routine would work, but he eventually regarded it as one of the funniest in the film.

Right: Boris Karloff in the 1941 Broadway production of Arsenic and Old Lace.

Left: Kenneth Williams as a vampiric mad scientist, with his prized creation, Oddbod, in Carry on Screaming.

BODY OF A BOY!
MIND OF A MONSTER!
SOUL OF AN UNEARTHLY THING!

I WAS A TEENAGE FRANKENSTEIN

starring

WHIT **BISSELL** · PHYLLIS **COATES** · Robert **BURTON** · Gary **CONWAY**

Produced by **HERMAN COHEN** · Directed by **HERBERT L. STROCK** · Screenplay by **KENNETH LANGTRY**

A JAMES H. NICHOLSON-SAMUEL Z. ARKOFF PRODUCTION · AN AMERICAN INTERNATIONAL PICTURE

Surely the best-loved comic version of the Frankenstein monster was created by Fred Gwynne in *The Munsters* (1964-6). One of the most famous TV series of all time, *The Munsters* was made by Kayro-Vue Productions, a subsidiary of Universal. It told the story of a family of strange and often hideous creatures who live a life of unconcerned abnormality in the middle of America. Interestingly, the Munster plot turns the original novel on its head, for the one beautiful member of the family is pitied by her relations as being hopelessly ugly by ghoulish standards. Although Fred Gwynne's makeup is an exaggerated version of Jack Pierce's original cinematic creature, his monster exudes a disarming sense of benignity.

Above: Abbot and Costello Meet Frankenstein, *a 1948 spoof with Glenn Strange as the monster, and a host of other stars from the Universal horror movies.*

Left: *The monster in* I Was a Teenage Frankenstein *was notable for its good looks – a teenager's head was grafted on to less youthful parts.*

Above left: *Kenneth Williams revitalizes Oddbod in* Carry On Screaming.

Below left: *Possibly the only musical Frankenstein film,* The Rocky Horror Picture Show *was made in 1975 and is now a cult movie. Frank N Furter (stunningly played by Tim Curry) gazes on his seven-day wonder, a gorgeous hunk of a monster created in only a week*

Above: *Goggle-eyed Marty Feldman as Igor, the hapless assistant in* Young Frankenstein. *He is possibly the only hunchback in cinematic history to have owned a moveable hump.*

Overleaf: *The Munsters, an all-American family of vampires, werewolves and monsters. Fred Gwynne played the entirely amiable monster, and Al Lewis a Dracula-related grandpa.*

Page 85: *Peter Boyle as the monster in* Young Frankenstein *(1974).*

Abbot and Costello was not the only comic film series to exploit the myth of *Frankenstein*. No doubt prompted as much by the Hammer series as by the Universal classics, Anglo-Amalgamated produced a *Frankenstein*-influenced addition to their dreadful Carry On series in 1966. *Carry On Screaming* featured a clumsy Frankensteinesque character in the form of Oddbod, although luckily both film and character rarely surface nowadays.

The wildest, wackiest, hippest production to feature a Frankenstein monster clone was surely *The Rocky Horror Picture Show*. This was first produced in 1973 on the stage of the tiny Royal Court theater in Sloane Square, London, but has now been staged all over the world.

The plot of the play had very little to do with the original *Frankenstein* story, and was really a skit on science-fiction teen movies. However, the most memorable character is Frank N Furter – a crazy monster figure who quickly became a cult personality in his own right. Tim Curry, who created the character on stage, went on to star in the massively successful film version produced by 20th Century Fox in 1975. Although *The Rocky Horror Picture Show* is not in any real sense a *Frankenstein* film, elements of the zany perverse humor that has made *Rocky Horror* such a lasting success can be traced back to the brilliant absurdity of the classic features directed by James Whale.

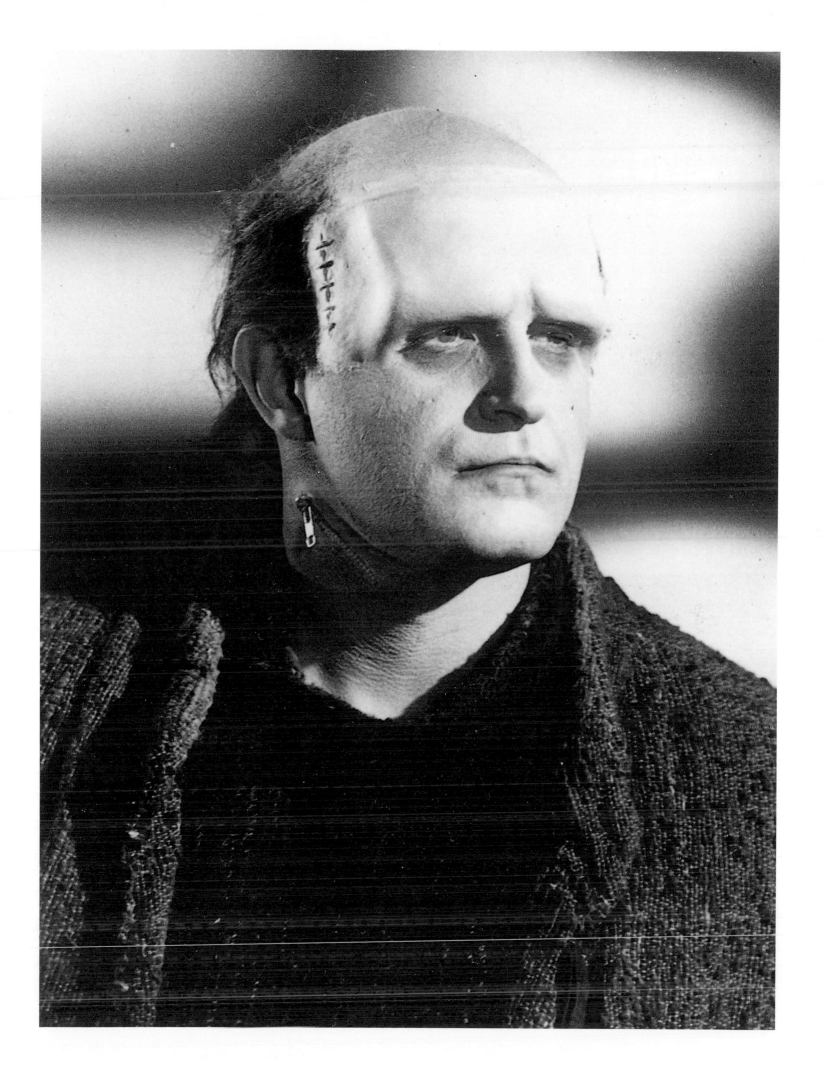

This is surely also true of the greatest monster comedy film to date – *Young Frankenstein*. This charming and hilarious movie was also made by 20th Century Fox in 1974, and featured the talents of Mel Brooks as director, the marvelous Gene Wilder as Dr Frederick Frankenstein, and Peter Boyle as the monster. Brooks slyly peppered the film with references to classic Hollywood horror films, so that any horror fan is tempted to play 'spot the quote' in between laughs. The film is deliberately and self-consciously 'show biz' (just like that other great film from the same stable, *The Producers*), and it is the cutting reception given to Frankenstein and the monster's ludicrous song-and-dance version of *Putting On The Ritz* that eventually sends the monster off on the rampage.

The film does have flaws, but it is churlish to pick on them. It is much more tempting to remember the magic moments – Marty Feldman's eyes looking like half-boiled eggs on a plate, the innocently crazy smiles of Gene Wilder, or the way Madeleine Kahn's hair goes frizzy after she has made love to the monster.

These pages: Mel Brooks' Young Frankenstein *is not only a glorious spoof on the horror movie genre, but also an affectionate tribute to the classic Frankensteins. Gene Wilder plays Frederick Frankenstein, a brilliant surgeon, and grandson of the infamous baron. Frederick is clearly sensitive about his heritage, and insists that his name be pronounced 'Fronkensteen'. On returning to his Transylvanian roots, however, he discovers both his grandfather's laboratory and his book, entitled* How I Did It. *Aided and abetted by Igor (Marty Feldman), he sets out to procure a body and a brain, and like his grandfather before him, creates a man-made monster. In a series of hilarious twists to the plot, the monster (Peter Boyle) falls in love with Frankenstein's frigid fiancée Elizabeth (Madeleine Kahn), which is fairly convenient for the good doctor, who has succumbed to the charms of the buxom Inga (Terri Garr).*

A Modern Myth

'Remember, I am not recording the vision of a madman.'

MARY SHELLEY, *Frankenstein*

I started by calling the story of *Frankenstein* a modern myth. But is it quite correct to call *Frankenstein* a myth? Or should we think of Mary Shelley's 'waking dream' as a *premonition*? Many people today are beginning to wonder whether the Frankenstein fiction is at last turning into fact. Certainly, if we repeated today the conversation Shelley and Byron ventured upon nearly two centuries ago, we might arrive at more informed, and perhaps more worrying, conclusions.

Peter Cushing, star of the Hammer Frankenstein films, noted in his memoirs that when musing on the character of Baron Frankenstein he liked to think of him as a predecessor of Dr Christiaan Barnard. Barnard, of course, was the first surgeon successfully to transplant a human heart.

Since Barnard transplant surgery has progressed apace. Kidneys, lungs and livers have all yielded to the advance of medical science. It has become a commonplace to hear of a friend's cornea replacement, or that some unlucky child's finger, or toe, or arm has been stitched back on by microsurgery. And now we have established the principle, it is surely only a matter of time until the holy grail is reached – a complete brain transplant!

And yet, and yet . . . the old fears awaken. Fear *for* the not-quite-dead and fear *of* the not-quite-alive. The peasants, as it were, start to mutter, and campaigns are mounted to regulate medical research, and to control the horrific organ-trade that is now growing between the developed and developing worlds. But perhaps we have become obsessed by the idea of losing bits of ourselves while we lie peacefully in a coma. For, as the old saying goes, there is more than one way of skinning a cat, and the scientist balked by legislation is liable to remember Frankenstein's last words: 'I have myself been blasted in these hopes, yet another may succeed.'

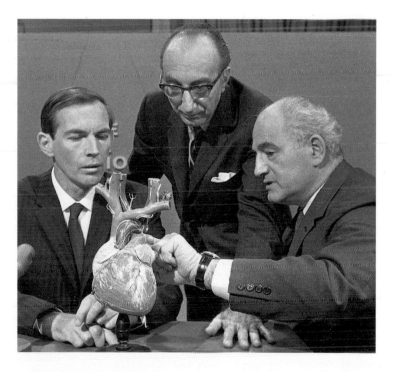

Left: *Boris Karloff, the classic monster, and an early fictional beneficiary of spare part surgery.*

Above: *Dr Christiaan Barnard, (left) who pioneered the first successful heart transplant.*

Left and below: *Stills from* Frankenstein: The True Story, *which illustrate the lengths to which early nineteenth century surgeons had to go in order to perform medical experiments on corpses. Even bona fide scientists found it hard to obtain bodies for medical purposes, and these pictures are not too much of an exaggeration of the truth.*

Right: *Dr Solomon Snyder displays a photograph of synthetically-grown brain cells, an interesting and sinister step forward.*

At present, there are at least two alternatives to the relatively crude method of actually stitching a human together from its constituent parts, as first outlined by Mary Shelley. The first of these is genetic engineering. For, once we have gained an understanding of the function of each element within our genetic make-up, and have perfected the nascent art of gene-splicing so that we can construct wholly artificial gene sequences, then mankind will be able not only to produce individual humans, but to grow whole armies of them. Already tissue technology enables doctors to grow human 'skin' for use on burn victims, revolutionizing their treatment. For some years now the Human Genome Project, which aims to catalog the function of each human gene, has been progressing in laboratories around the world. The fundamental genetic library at his disposal, the 'mad scientist' of the twenty-first century will be able to design his latest creation without having to go anywhere near a messy operating table.

The second 'monster building' method skips all the immensely complex biological and moral problems that are liable to bog down the surgical and genetic options. It is, of course, the idea of building an entirely artificial intelligence.

Science fiction writers have toyed for decades with the 'android' concept, but it is only in the last few years that we have seen the first primitive examples beginning to appear in research laboratories across the world. These prototypes have yet to attain the intelligence of the Universal monster, and are mental pygmies compared to Mary Shelley's devious wretch. Yet the leap-frogging advances being made in computing, with each generation of machine now being used to help design its successor, suggest that a true artificial intelligence will be attained within the next two decades.

And what then? What exactly shall we say to it? How shall we treat it? Perhaps we shall find, despite Mary Shelley's 200-year-old warning, that in our lust for power and knowledge we have created a new being without the slightest thought for the future of either it or ourselves. Perhaps, even, we shall begin to long for the days when *Frankenstein* could be thought of as just a modern myth.

And perhaps, after an interval, like Frankenstein himself on the glacier at Chamonix, we shall be forced to contemplate the recent wreckage of our world and wonder bitterly 'What are the duties of a creator towards his creature?'

Left: A nineteenth century engraving of the gruesome habit of bodysnatching.

Right: Christiaan Barnard (left) advises a team of Turkish surgeons during a heart-transplant operation.

Below: The modern method of creating beings. Advances in microchip technology mean that fully-fledged robots or androids will probably exist within the next two decades.

Overleaf: A dramatic still from The Cabinet of Dr Caligari. The somnambulist, under the influence of an evil hypnotist, carries the heroine across the roof tops.

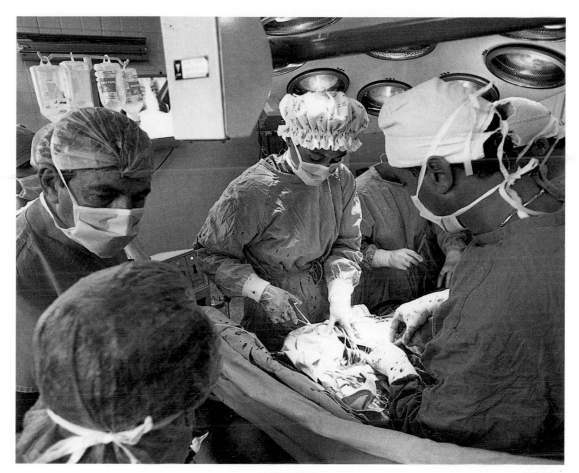

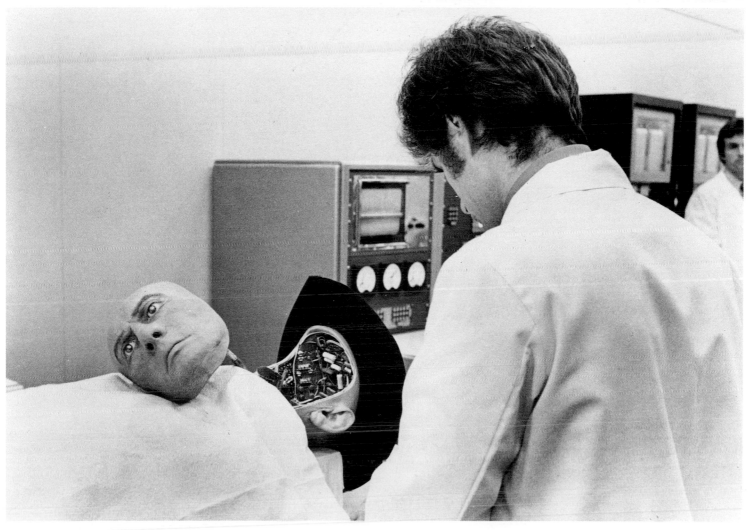